Going the Extra Mile:
University of Rhode Island
Engineers in the Global Workplace

Dedicated to

Heidi Kirk Duffy
Chairperson of the
IEP Advisory Board

Out of gratitude for a quarter century
of encouragement and support

Going the Extra Mile:
University of Rhode Island Engineers in the Global Workplace

by

John M. Grandin

Publication by Rockland Press
Wakefield, Rhode Island 2011
Inquiries: grandin@uri.edu

Cover photo of Berlin Reichstag
by IEP student
Payam Fahr

Printed by CreateSpace.Com
ISBN: 978-1466391314

Contents

Preface   8

Introduction (goals and methodology)   10

IEP (program overview and history)   16

Johnathan DiMuro
BS Chemical Engineering; BA German   25

Eric McCoy Sargent
BS Mechanical Engineering; BA German
Dual Degree MS/Diplom Program, URI,
Technische Universität Braunschweig   35

Ana Catalina Franco
BS Mechanical Engineering; BA German   48

Jesse Michael Schneider
BS Mechanical Engineering and German   60

Sonia Gaitan
BS Chemical Engineering; BA Spanish
with Portuguese   70

Christina and Michael Smith
BS Mechanical and Electrical Engineering;
BA German   79

Daniel Fischer
BS Electrical Engineering; BA German   91

Sharon Ruggieri
BS Mechanical Engineering; BA Spanish   100

Matthew Zimmerman
BS Ocean Engineering; BA French and
German   111

Nika McManus
BS Mechanical Engineering; BA German
Dual Degree MS/Diplom Program, URI,
Technische Universität Braunschweig   119

Sareh Rajaee
BS Biomedical Engineering; BA German   129

Ryan Cournoyer
BS Civil Engineering; BA French   138

Peter Alberg
BS Mechanical Engineering; BA German   147

Peter Wiedenhoff
Diplom Wirtschaftsingenieurwesen; Dr.-Ing.,
Technische Universität Braunschweig
MBA, University of Rhode Island   155

Conclusions   164

About the author   179

The best educators understand that "extra" and "creativity" are not so much taught as they are unlocked and let out, after which they are usually self-propelled.

Thomas Friedman and Michael Mandelbaum[1]

---

[1] Friedman, Thomas and Mandelbaum, Michael, <u>That Used to be Us</u>, Farrar, Straus, and Giroux, New York, 2011, page 148.

Preface

After 23 years of encouraging University of Rhode Island engineering students to acquire a second language along with their technical studies, and to study and intern abroad before entering the workplace, I felt it was time to ask some of our alumni who pursued this course of study what difference it has made for their careers. I am now retired and have the freedom to do this, and, happily, have a strong enough relationship with our former students to count on their honest, open, and thoughtful responses to my inquiries. This study focuses, therefore, on the education and early professional development of fourteen graduates of URI's International Engineering Program (IEP), a well established curriculum through which students simultaneously earn both an engineering and a language degree (BS/BA) over five years and spend their entire fourth academic year studying and interning abroad. Also included, in order to provide a view from another direction, is the story of a German engineering alumnus who spent a year as an exchange student at URI and currently works as a business and engineering consultant in Munich.

Though still relatively early in their personal and professional lives, these fifteen young engineers have each achieved substantial success since graduation. While they were all good students based on any standard measurement, and were thus candidates for success with or without the IEP, they nevertheless share a bond as fellow IEP graduates and believe strongly that the program provided them with a unique set of skills beyond the traditional engineering education, and that these have played a significant role in preparing them for their achievements. My intent is to examine the extent to which this is truly the case, i.e., to ask if, how, and why their international education has made a difference in their careers. It is hoped that the resulting series of case studies will help us all to appreciate and better understand the value and nature of an in-depth international education, i.e., the extent to which significant time spent abroad is, as is often claimed, a life-changing and door-opening experience, as well as a desirable and valuable ingredient for professional success in today's global work-place. I hope not only to be able to more clearly define the outcomes of the URI International Engineering Program curriculum, but also to exploit and share their implications for future program development, at URI and elsewhere.

John Grandin
Ocean Park, Maine
Fall 2011

Introduction

In this era of globalization, when the American economy is so clearly challenged by developing nations such as India, China, and Brazil, it is now broadly recognized that American students must be educated more rigorously, more competitively, and more internationally. This means higher standards in math, science, and engineering; it also means preparing young Americans in all subject areas to work in culturally and linguistically diverse settings. It is not surprising, therefore, that higher education leaders are paying far more attention to global education. It is also not surprising that American parents now clearly have "international" on their shopping list as they look for the right college or university for their offspring.

It is furthermore a sign of the times that engineering educators have joined those stressing the importance of international education, a phenomenon traditionally reserved for humanities students, especially language majors and especially women. The message from business and industry has become loud and clear. Technological and scientific leadership, predominantly and comfortably in the hands of Americans in the decades after World War II, are now global undertakings, with many companies combing the world for talent, manufacturing advantage, and even conducting research and development across multiple boundaries. Engineering graduates, therefore, must be prepared to work in many different national locations, with peers who hail from very different cultural settings, and in many cases have very different values, priorities, tastes, problem solving patterns, and very different styles of communication.[2]

As a result of these global shifts, it is not uncommon for engineering deans to cite global education as a higher priority for their majors and, for example, to monitor the numbers of their students going abroad. Colleges of engineering have created associate deanships for international education; partnerships have been formed with engineering colleagues abroad, and many international engineering education models have evolved at universities across the country, enabling students, for example, to study or intern abroad or work with peers at distant universities on common technical projects. Renssellaer Polytechnic Institute, for example, has mandated that all of its students study abroad during their undergraduate years; Brigham Young University has announced a $10,000,000 gift in support of a new Center for Global Leadership; Georgia Institute of Technology has created an International Plan which gives their students the opportunity to combine engineering and other fields with language study and experiences abroad; parallel to its International Engineering Program, the University of Rhode Island supports this trend in the profession with an annual conference focused on the issues of international engineering education and an on-line journal providing an outlet for the dissemination of relevant ideas and best practices.[3]

While engineering educators may rightfully be proud of the progress made in the last decade in preparing students to work internationally, many would concur, especially when compared with the global preparation of engineering students in other countries, that only baby steps have been

---

[2] David Weidman, CEO of Celanese Corporation, illustrated this point when speaking to attendees of the 14th Annual Colloquium on International Engineering Education, held November 2011 at Brigham Young University. In his words, Celanese will not hire engineers who do not provide evidence of "global agility" in support of a strong technical expertise.
[3] For additional information on the Annual Colloquium and the Online Journal, see: http://www.uri.edu/iep

taken in the American system. Of all American students studying abroad in 2010 (approximately 271,000), just 3.9% (10,554) were engineers.[4] If one considers that there are approximately 450,000 students enrolled in undergraduate engineering programs in the U.S.,[5] this means that just 2% of engineering students studied abroad in that year. These figures become even more discouraging if one considers that only 3.9% of all American students participating in organized programs abroad stay for a full academic year, with over one half doing just a summer or other short-term program.[6]

There is, furthermore, little agreement as to our basic understanding of the requirements for the international preparation of engineering students. Despite the increase in programs and models and the growth in numbers of engineering students being sent abroad, engineering educators are far from sure about the best ways to achieve a global education for their students. Indeed, there is a lack of clarity about the very goals of international education and how to demonstrate that those goals have been met. What are the characteristics of a globally educated engineer? What are the characteristics of a good global education program for engineers? Is such training necessary for all engineering students, or just for a select few? How do we know if the goals have been achieved? And, if they have been achieved what difference does it make? Although there is broad support for the global education of engineers at the instinctual level, it is based largely upon anecdotal evidence. Uncertainty about the details still prevails.

Measuring the effectiveness of sending students abroad, whether it be for a summer study program, a study tour to China, a semester or year-long program is extremely difficult. While we can measure math skills, language

---

[4] Data is taken from the 2011 Open Doors report of the Institute of International Education.

[5] Data is taken from 2010 ASEE Profiles of Engineering and Engineering Technology Colleges, American Society for Engineering Education.

[6] Data is taken from the 2011 Open Doors report of the Institute of International Education.

12

acquisition, the ability to solve physics problems, the ability to conduct and conclude a research project, the tools are hardly there to assess the extent to which students have acquired the ability to work in a global setting, even among international education specialists. The question remains how universities may best assess where and how to efficiently and wisely invest resources in international education programs for undergraduates. Institutions are nevertheless moving forward with their programs, with the belief that study abroad, work abroad, and travel abroad are inherently good. As mentioned above, some institutions have even mandated international study experiences for their students.

This volume will address the issues associated with the goals and effectiveness of a global engineering education based upon an in-depth study of fifteen graduates of one of the nation's most distinctive and recognized programs of this nature, the International Engineering Program (IEP) at the University of Rhode Island. Each of these former students spent an additional year as part of his or her undergraduate program, each learned a second or, in some cases, third language (German, French, Spanish, Chinese), each spent an entire year abroad, studying at a partner university and interning with a cooperating company. Our study will seek to determine what they gained from this extra commitment at the bachelor level, what difference it has made for their lives and careers now that they are practicing professionals, and what implications this information has as we move forward with future curricular planning.

This study will not be based on scientific measurement instruments and/or, as might be expected, a broad statistical review of all 350 graduates of the IEP. I have, rather, selected a small cross-section of young professionals, all of whom completed URI's extensive international training along with their engineering education, and who have achieved success in the workplace. Their stories will be based upon the results of a questionnaire and in-depth personal interviews. Conclusions will be drawn regarding

13

the outcomes of the URI model, and, in each case, I will ask what we as educators can learn from these former students.

Though the number of cases in this study is small, the group as a whole is very unique. Intelligent, gifted, and well motivated, it is safe to say that each of these alums would have found his or her way to professional achievement with or without an international component in the course of study. Each had planned to study engineering as an undergraduate, and would not have done the language degree or the year abroad, had the very unusual program not presented itself to them at URI. In other words, they were pre-committed engineering students who opted freely for a curriculum which added a year of study, gave them a second or third language and a study and a work experience abroad. It is thus very appropriate, now that they have been in the workplace for a number of years, to seek to determine the extent to which their international education experiences provided additional value and, therefore, helped, enhanced, accelerated or possibly hindered their personal and professional growth. Simply put, if the program has made a difference, how and why is this the case? What did they gain, or lose, as a result of the totality of this unusual and demanding undergraduate curriculum over and above that which the engineering education would have offered by itself? What additional soft skills and hard skills did they acquire through their international education? What added value did the IEP provide and what role does that play in their careers? Furthermore, if the program was effective, what features or aspects of the program had the most significant impact?

In preparation for the narratives about each of the fifteen alums, I asked them in detail where they are today, what their positions are and have been, how they have gotten where they are and what aspects of their successes they believe may be attributed to the IEP. I asked them to look back and reflect on their international education in hopes that we may gain a better understanding of the overall outcomes of such a program. In the process, I have also sought to determine what we as educators can learn from

14

them that may influence our thinking as we plan and set our own priorities for the future.

By probing their experiences and their lives, I sought also to understand the extent to which personality or early life experiences might predispose one to opt for such a program of study, which might point to the likelihood of success in the global workplace. What makes one likely to be an IEP student? Is it personality? Do teachers make the difference? Parents? High school trips abroad? This relatively small number of case studies will not suffice to answer all our questions, but they will contribute to our understanding of the nature and value of global education as practiced at URI. We hope that it will provide evidence of the extent of its value and guidance for the process of continuous program improvement.

I regret that this volume does not include any case studies for students completing the IEP curriculum with Chinese as the language. The latter program is much more recent in its development. Though its first students graduated in 2011, there are no Chinese IEPers with a history in the workplace (yet!).

Readers will also note that the cases presented are dominated by former German IEP students, with a smaller number from the Spanish and French programs. This reflects the historical development of the IEP, which began exclusively as a German and Engineering program, with French and then Spanish added as the second and third language options, to be followed more recently by Mandarin Chinese.

IEP

The International Engineering Program (IEP) at the University of Rhode Island is a five-year undergraduate program leading simultaneously to both the Bachelor of Science in any one of the engineering disciplines and the Bachelor of Arts in German, French, Spanish, and, most recently, also in Chinese.[7] Students study the language and its related culture(s) each semester along with their engineering curriculum, and spend the entire fourth year abroad, completing one semester of study at a partner university and a six-month professional internship with a cooperating company. Features of the program include content-based language courses for engineers, summer internship opportunities with global companies in the U.S., as well as six-month internships abroad, and extensive corporate contacts for post-graduate career placement. The goal is to graduate engineering students with a high level of competency in a second language as well as significant practical engineering experience in a different cultural setting.

When IEP students go abroad, in most cases they first attend a partner university for one semester, where they are expected to do additional language and culture study, at least one engineering course, and an engineering research project in a university research institute. While some of the

---

[7] More extensive information about the University of Rhode Island International Engineering Program may be found in articles by John M. Grandin available through the Online Journal for Global Engineering Education at: http://digitalcommons.uri.edu/ojgee/. For details, see pages 180 - 182.

16

coursework is done in a language-sheltered mode, meaning that the course is taught for foreign students and not native speakers, all work is nevertheless done in French, German, Spanish, or Mandarin Chinese. Living accommodations follow the standards of the partner university, with housing in dormitories or privately in apartments with native speakers. IEP students do not live together with other Americans. Orientation and advising are conducted by partner faculty or staff at the guest university. Out of principle there are no URI faculty or advisers on location.

The second part of the year abroad is comprised of a paid six-month internship experience with a partner company in the country of the target language and culture. The IEP assists with the location and application process for the internship, although the application itself is prepared by the students in the language and appropriate style. It is made clear to students and company mentors that any work related to the internship may not be conducted in English. The internship is designed to be a professional engineering experience, related to the student's major field of study, with specifically designed goals. Although each case is different, the companies generally provide housing or at least assistance with the search for housing and all offer a monthly subsistence stipend.

The IEP has enjoyed considerable growth and success over its twenty-four year history, having now graduated over 350 students, many of whom have put their global skills to work. Twenty-five percent of all engineering undergrads at URI are currently enrolled in the IEP; approximately thirty-five IEP students are sent abroad each year, completing their semester of study and their six-month internship. The program attracts highly motivated and talented students, the majority of whom are supported at least partially by honors scholarships.

The IEP has also impacted engineering education at the graduate level through the introduction of dual degree masters and doctoral programs in partnership with the Technical University of Braunschweig in Germany. The dual degree graduate programs have been very popular with

German students, with 160 MS or MBA degrees awarded to Braunschweig students by the University of Rhode Island. American students have also been attracted to the program, even if only gradually, with seventeen URI dual degrees completed or in progress.[8]

The IEP leadership has maintained the consistent position that international education cannot be taken lightly or be satisfied through any form of short-term experience, as is often the case at other institutions across the country. (The IIE Open Doors report shows that 56.6% of American students studying abroad participate in a summer or other short-term program while 39.4%% are abroad for one semester; only 3.9% participate in full-year programs.) It has also been clear in its commitment to language education as a key part of the preparation, strongly disagreeing with the argument that the "whole world speaks English," and that native speakers of English do not need to be bilingual. The IEP is a totally integrated experience, beginning on day-one of the freshman year and including a full year abroad, the completion of two majors and two degree programs (BA/BS) over the five-year period. IEP students are expected not just to take language courses, but to become highly proficient in the language. When abroad they take engineering courses and conduct research in the language; they are expected to complete a professional internship in a company setting where the target language is the primary source of communication. The IEP is built on the belief that students cannot penetrate or appreciate the thinking and the engineering culture of their host country without being able to speak and understand the native language. It is also based on the belief that multilingualism has become a worldwide standard and is a mark of an educated person in the global workplace.

---

[8] See: "International Dual Degrees at the Graduate Levels: The University of Rhode Island and the Technische Universität Braunschweig," in the Online Journal for Global Engineering Education, Volume 3, Issue 1, Fall 2008.

The IEP has a dedicated and professional staff who mentor and guide its students and work closely with both engineering and language faculty to ensure an effective and fully integrated education. The program enjoys a complex of two former fraternity houses serving as both its administrative and residential center, and named for the chairperson of the IEP Advisory Board, Heidi Kirk Duffy, to whom this volume is dedicated. The IEP House and Texas Instruments House offer a home base to all IEP students and faculty, and house 76 IEP students. The IEP has its own dining room and full-time kitchen staff and serves meals each day to its residents, as well as other students and faculty in the program. The center is a living and learning community, featuring specialized language floors, study groups, and tutoring. Several of the residents are engineering exchange students from partner universities in Germany, France, Spain, Mexico, and China.

A major role for the IEP directorship is corporate relations. This is done first of all to ensure that students will have internship positions abroad. But the program also seeks steady input from the private sector to keep itself on track for real world needs, and also to provide its graduates with networking for employment upon graduation. With their added value, IEP graduates tend to be very much in demand and the rate of employment at graduation is very close to 100%.

The IEP director and staff work hard to stay in touch with graduates of the program. This is never a perfect process, since young professionals often move from one position to the other. But the record keeping is simplified by the fact that IEP students tend to have a special identity as such; they see themselves as a special group and many maintain close post-graduate contact with each other and the IEP home base, whether by traditional modes or modern social networking programs such as Facebook.

Most IEP graduates go to work as engineers with global companies, whether American or foreign-based. Several have gone on to impressive graduate programs in engineering, at schools such as MIT, Princeton, Yale, and

Georgia Tech. Some have taken other professional routes, becoming math and science teachers, going on to top MBA programs, law schools, or even medical school. And some have postponed their first career step by joining the military or the Peace Corps or, in two cases, hiking the Appalachian Trail. Several are working for companies abroad, while many are working for the U.S. subsidiaries of foreign companies or American companies with significant commitments overseas. Others have gone to work for organizations with no specific foreign obligations. And still others have founded their own start-up companies. It has become clear to us that recruiters value IEP graduates whether they need them for global work or not. IEP graduates are seen as impressive young people who have shown a determination to go the extra mile; they are seen as highly motivated students, with significant added value and strong communication abilities; they are easily identified as risk takers and young engineers with definite leadership potential.

In selecting the IEP alumni to be the focus of this volume, I have admittedly, for reasons given above, chosen several success stories, but at the same time have maintained program diversity from several perspectives. Of the fifteen, fourteen are Americans and one is a German who spent a year at URI as an IEP exchange student. Four of the group are currently living and working abroad, while nine are employed by global companies in the U.S.; two are currently in graduate school. Of the fifteen, four are working for companies in Germany, four are employed by foreign-owned companies in the U.S., four are working for U.S. firms with global interests, one has founded his own start-up company with a global reach, one is in graduate school pursuing an MBA, and one is in medical school. Ten of the alumni represent the German IEP, which is the original language of the program and still maintains its flagship role; two are grads of the Spanish program and one of the French IEP, while one of the group completed both the French and German programs; yet another was an exchange student from Germany who completed the MBA at URI. Six alums represented here are women; two are Hispanic, one was

Russian born and another born in Iran. Each of these students is highly motivated and hard working. They are likewise equally thoughtful about their choices and their life's goals. I consider myself fortunate, as their former mentor and IEP Director, to be able to call upon them for their thoughts and am grateful for their willing participation in this project.

Before introducing you to these fifteen special persons, however, it is important that I explain my own background with the IEP and explain my qualifications for approaching this task. Readers will note that I, as a language professional, will have an obvious prejudice regarding the role of language study and use in the process. Yet, I hope to be as objective as possible in my study, in order to provide information of value to a broad range of educators in the higher education community.

I am by training and title a Professor of German language and literature and served at the University of Rhode Island in that capacity for forty years until my retirement in 2010. I taught German language at all levels and originally enjoyed a research focus on Franz Kafka who lived and wrote in Prague in the late nineteenth and early twentieth centuries. Before launching the IEP, I also served for four years as Associate Dean and one year as Acting Dean of the URI College of Arts and Sciences. Midway in my career at URI, however, my professional life took on a totally new dimension, when I was able to join with the Dean of Engineering at that time, Dr. Hermann Viets, to put forward the concept of the IEP. Funded by a grant from the U.S. Department of Education, we launched the program in 1987 with an immediate positive student response. I thus became the co-founder of the IEP and then served for over 23 years as its developer, director, and champion.

Though I valued my training as a literary scholar and my early career at URI, I was very aware of the fact that interest in language learning among American students was waning. I was also troubled by the fact that the American university model for language learning was rooted exclusively in the study of national literatures, and basically lacked any applications at the advanced levels for students of other disciplines. When given the chance, therefore, I welcomed the opportunity to collaborate with engineering and design a program that would attract bright students from outside the traditional humanities tracks.

The IEP was built on the observation that the world of business and technology was becoming more and more international and that engineering students would need special training for that reality. Hermann Viets and I were of one mind that this was an important step to take and we both agreed that language should play an important role. Thus evolved the idea of the simultaneous study of both language and engineering, reinforced by an extensive period abroad, all of which would lead to two bachelor degrees over five years: the BA in a language and the BS in an engineering discipline.

As director of the IEP, my role at URI grew far beyond that of a traditional language professor. My first task was to develop special sections of German language classes for students of engineering, in which technical content materials would be integrated with the traditional learning process. Our goal would be to motivate students to stay with the program by relating language learning directly to their primary professional interests. Secondly, I needed to develop a program of outreach to business and industry to ensure that IEP students would have professional internship opportunities following their first three years of study. Thirdly, we needed to develop a relationship with a technical university in Germany, to open the door for study abroad, for student exchange and for eventual dual degree programs. Beyond these basic responsibilities for the development of the IEP, I needed to serve as mentor and advisor for the students in the program. They required advice, help, and encouragement at many stages, but most critically, they needed help to arrange their six-month internships abroad and their semester of study abroad.

My role as director tended to grow more complex each year, often by leaps and bounds. The IEP offered assistance with domestic as well as foreign internships, and with eventual job placement. Once our model for the German IEP was well established, the program then grew to include a French model, then a Spanish IEP and eventually a Chinese program. This was followed by our forays into the housing and dining program, with the takeover and reno-vation of the two fraternity houses mentioned above, the IEP House and the Texas Instruments House. As a result of the complexity and totally integrated nature of the program, I came to know each of the students in the program quite well, and this can certainly be said of the fifteen alumni represented in this study. Though I knew some better than others, I played a role for each of them and have followed their progress through the steps of the IEP and since graduation as well.

Over the years I have become nationally and internationally involved in the globalization of engineering education and have spoken and published widely on the topic. I am also founder of the sole annual conference devoted strictly to the issues associated with the global education of engineers, the Annual Colloquium on Inter-national Engineering Education, which will enjoy its fif-teenth year in 2012.[9] And my colleagues and I are responsible for the sole professional journal devoted exclu-sively to these issues, the Online Journal for Global Engineering Education.[10]

My own involvement with the students during the course of their undergraduate years has given me a closer personal relationship with most than is traditional in any higher education environment. As a result of my role as director of the program, and developer of the IEP living/learning community, it has been relatively uncomp-licated and even natural to follow the students in their careers and to be able to approach them now for this study. Fortunately, this relationship enables me to penetrate beyond the surface with my questions, which are, to a degree, rather personal. My assumption is that we will not

---

[9] See: http://www.uri.edu/iep/colloquia
[10] See: http://digitalcommons.uri.edu/ojgee

fully understand how and why international education makes a difference without looking at the persons involved, their personalities and character traits, the influences that made a difference for them, the steps that they took and the people who helped them. While it might be easy to explain how the IEP has supported them in their career paths, it is much more difficult to explain why they wanted and opted for the program, and why they were good candidates for international careers. It is also important at this stage to understand the extent to which the program has impacted their personal lives, indeed their personalities, as well as their careers. In each of the case studies, therefore, I will attempt to look beyond the obvious in my analysis of their success. In each of the case studies I will also ask what, specifically, we as educators can learn from them.

Note: This study was undertaken during the 2011 calendar year and represents a snapshot view of the dynamic lives and careers of these IEP graduates, which will most certainly continue to evolve. Indeed, some have already reported to me that their jobs are changing, i.e., they have been promoted or have decided to move on to the next stage in their careers. Readers need to be aware, therefore, that the stories told will continue to be valid for the goals of this study as they are, even though they are incomplete.

Johnathan DiMuro

I'm a much different person as a result of the IEP. The world is a lot smaller and my ambitions are a lot larger. Challenges do not look as daunting, and as a result, I'm more willing and able to provide my opinion or step forward to work on a project.

I would have never considered going abroad before the IEP, and now country borders are blurred in my mind.

Born: 1980 in New Jersey, raised in Rhode Island;

High School: Cumberland, Rhode Island;

IEP Degrees: BA in German; BS in Chemical Engineering, 2003

Graduate Degrees: Masters of Philosophy in Engineering for Sustainable Development, Cambridge-MIT Institute, Centre for Sustainable Development, University of Cambridge, Cambridge, England, 2006. Supported by Truman Fellowship

Current position: Project Manager, Ecosystem Services, Sustainability and Environment, Health & Safety (EH&S), The Dow Chemical Company, Midland, Michigan

Past Positions: Research and Development Engineer, Parlex, Inc., Cranston, RI (2003-2005); Improvement Engineer (2006-2008), Innovation Engineer (2008-2010), Environmental Technology Center, The Dow Chemical Company

Personal: Married, with two children

In January 2011, The Dow Chemical Company and The Nature Conservancy announced a collaboration that intends to revolutionize the chemical industry's relationship to the environment in every aspect of its business. Funded with an initial $10,000,000 investment from Dow, and a commitment of expertise from the Conservancy, this Fortune 50 company and its NGO collaborator launched a major business initiative at the Dow headquarters in Michigan to oversee its commitment to sustainability, whether in terms of plant location, manufacturing practice, product development, or any other business consideration for all of its operations worldwide in 37 countries. Much to the pride of the URI International Engineering Program, the Project Leader for Ecosystem Services in this Division of Sustainability, Environment, Health and Safety is Johnathan DiMuro who graduated from URI in 2003 with degrees in chemical engineering and German.

John DiMuro has been concerned with the world about him since childhood. Whether helping the local and at that time controversial hospice for AIDS victims in his home town or getting involved with the restoration of the nearby Blackstone River, or, as an undergrad, leading the House Council of the IEP House living and learning community, John has always felt the need to be a productive part of the world around him and to consider the long-term implications of current actions or policies. Sustainability has become a watchword for him, and his current position is a logical outcome for his own highest principles. The IEP is gratified that it played a role in helping him get to this level of achievement at a relatively young age and we are happy to tell at least a part of his story here.

Like almost each of the others in this study, the IEP became the single most important differentiator for John when choosing his undergraduate school. As a strong student in high school with a concern for the environment, he knew he wanted a science program, but assumed that a quality education could only be found at a private school. At the same time, he was looking for a "non-cookie-cutter" approach to his education and a challenge beyond the standard curriculum. Before making a decision after being admitted to several schools, John's father convinced him to take a look at his state university, which he did "kicking and screaming," since he had applied to URI only as his back-up school. But, as he tells us, that day changed his life. First of all he heard a presentation by Professor Vincent Rose at the Chemical Engineering Department asserting that "the future of the environment and chemistry would not be in cleaning up pollution once it had occurred, but developing technology that would eliminate it from being formed in the first place," an argument that made enormous sense to him. On the same day, he learned about the IEP and met with a student studying chemical engineering and German, who was soon to go to Germany for a year of study and a professional internship. He was glad to have the chance to spend a day with her, attending classes and getting to know the program through the eyes of those in mid-stream. Given

27

his enthusiasm for language studies after learning Spanish for five years, and the possibility of doing language and culture coursework alongside engineering, and spending his fourth year abroad, John opted without further consideration for URI and the IEP.

John became a fully engaged member of the URI and IEP community while an undergraduate. He was a member of the rowing team, a charter resident of the IEP House living and learning community and a leader of its House Council governing board. He worked closely with the faculty and played consistent roles in helping to improve the program and shape its policies. John also took advantage of internship opportunities, working in local business and industry each summer before going to Germany. At the same time, he sang each week in a semi-professional church choir in Providence, keeping his commitment to spirituality and the arts very much alive alongside his rigorous and demanding academic program.

Based upon his strong record, the unusual nature of the IEP itself, and his interest in sustainable development, John was encouraged in his third year at URI to make application for a scholarship for graduate study from the Harry S. Truman Foundation. This highly competitive program recognizes "college juniors with exceptional leadership potential who are committed to careers in government, the nonprofit or advocacy sectors, education or elsewhere in the public service." John was indeed selected as a Truman Scholar, and this fact helped him to secure admission and to finance his post-graduate study at Cambridge University in England where he would earn the Masters of Philosophy in Engineering for Sustainable Development.

In the wake of the Truman competition, John went first to Germany for his fourth year of undergraduate study. Typical of John he was able to find housing on his own with four German students rather than staying in the dormitory in Braunschweig. This enabled him to be in an environment where only German was spoken and where he could get closer to the day-to-day culture and learn how German students lived and what they thought and talked about. This experience was particularly good, since it enabled him to see how informed Europeans tend to be about world affairs; it also enabled him to see firsthand the extent to which Germans are committed to environmental stewardship and recycling. Given the value of this living environment and the good experience he was having as a research assistant at Braunschweig's Institute for Chemical and Thermal Process Engineering, John spent his full academic year in Braunschweig, rather than transitioning at mid-year to an industrial internship. At the institute, he was an assistant researcher for Volker Höfling, a post-doctoral student, conducting research on heat exchanger fouling under various conditions, in an effort to discover a way to prevent or minimize it. Results of his work and experiments were incorporated into international presentations and publications as part of Höfling's body of work.

When graduating in 2003 with his degrees in German and Chemical Engineering, John could have gone directly to graduate school, but decided to first gain some experience in industry. He therefore went to work in Rhode Island as a Research and Development Engineer for Parlex, in Cranston, RI. There he did research in advanced technology for printed circuit manufacturing, including Radio Frequency Identification (RFID) Tags, Organic LED (OLED), advanced reliability and performance of products, and also worked to reduce "bottlenecks" in the manufacturing process to increase production. But this was temporary for John who was still eager to get more deeply involved in public policy issues as they impact sustainable manufacturing and who in the meantime had been accepted into the special program for this topic at Cambridge University.

John tells us that he never would have considered graduate study abroad, had it not been for the IEP. Nor does he think he would have been competitive for a Truman Scholarship without the distinctive nature of the IEP. Both became a reality, however, and he did spend the 2005-2006 academic year at Cambridge's Centre for Sustainable

Development. There he studied under the direction of both Cambridge and Massachusetts Institute of Technology professors, learning how to integrate his knowledge of engineering into the larger challenge of sustainability. The program broadened his engineering skills through leadership, business, economics, environmental and policy courses that focused on the challenges facing the public and private sectors as they seek to balance profit, people, and planet, the "triple bottom line" of sustainability. John finished his year in defense of his thesis on the "Effectiveness of National Policies at Reducing Exhaust Pollution from Automobile Transportation." Taking a page from his IEP experience, he conducted his research on not one, but multiple countries: Germany, the United Kingdom, and the United States.

John toyed with the idea of finding a position with a public policy agency or think-tank after the year in Cambridge, but opted to go once again to industry, hoping to be able to impact policy from within. This time he joined one of the giants in the chemical industry, finding a position as Improvement Engineer in the Environmental Technology Center of The Dow Chemical Company in Freeport, Texas. In this position he was responsible for identifying solutions for the environmental units (wastewater, water supply, landfill) and for decreasing the operational cost while improving performance. In his first two years, he was able to develop solutions that would save the company over $10 million in Net Present Value. In 2008 John was promoted to Innovation Engineer at the same location where he was responsible for developing and implementing future environmental technologies. Such technologies included new ways to destroy byproducts through gasification, and a new analysis technique to determine the total environmental impact of a process change. In 2011 John was promoted to his current position as Project Manager in the new Dow collaboration with The Nature Conservancy.

Although John has very limited opportunity to use his German language skills or his specific German culture expertise, he is called upon each day to put his cross-cultural knowledge to use. Dow Chemical operates in 37 countries

30

and his work at Dow, which has always intersected with colleagues at other locations around the world, now must be integrated with all Dow divisions in all 37 countries. John is very accustomed to working in multi-locational global teams and, as is the case for so many of the others in this study, is very familiar with the conference calls that must be held in the early morning or late evening hours to coordinate with different time zones. And he is accustomed and attuned to the fact that what is verbally stated and agreed upon in such meetings is not necessarily equally understood by all or that seemingly simple words like "yes" do not necessarily have the same meaning from one culture to the next. In his words: *I am much more aware of culture, non-verbal communication, and the confusion that may arise from language or cultural differences than I would have been otherwise (without the IEP). Dow has manufacturing facilities in 37 countries, so cross-cultural communication is a very important part of my job. It's critical to being a good team leader, or even a team participant.*

John certainly has no regrets about the IEP, its extra work and its extra time. Somewhat like we will see in the case of Sharon Ruggieri, he feels that entry into the IEP set off a chain reaction in his undergraduate years, leading him to his current place in his career. The unique curriculum, in conjunction with his excellent record of achievement, distinguished him from others when applying for the Truman Scholarship or admission to Cambridge University for the masters program. The IEP, with its year abroad, exposure to his field in depth in Germany as well as the U.S., made him more employable, opened more doors for him, with the combination of all of things leading to a fine position with Dow Chemical and then the Project Manager for Dow's new collaboration with The Nature Conservancy.

What can we learn from Johnathan DiMuro?
1. As we will see with others in this study, the IEP with its global curriculum has become a magnet for attracting, encouraging and nurturing gifted students with broad interests and abilities. Johnathan DiMuro

has established his record as a scientist and engineer, but this is only part of his platform. Given his own nature, coupled with his exposure to the larger world, John sees the big picture and is not afraid to ask about the wider implications of his work or the work of those in his field. This is further rounded and impacted by his interests in the arts, music, and world affairs, much of which unfortunately rarely enters the workplace and the realm of those making major decisions. Higher education and the IEP need to take note of the fact that curricula such as this can play a major role in the development of future leaders. The IEP can and should promote itself as a track for a next generation of liberally educated leaders.

2. The IEP and URI need to take note of the importance and value of outreach and recruitment programs. The University of Rhode Island had been John's last choice until he got to campus, heard Professor Rose speak, and met with then undergraduate IEP student Tonya McBride. Had he not been approached personally, had he not visited campus, had he not learned personally of the IEP, he would not have come to URI. That would have been unfortunate for him and for the University of Rhode Island.

3. As is the case with all of our IEP alums in this volume, John has the characteristics of a leader and would most certainly have been successful with or without the IEP. He makes it clear, however, that the IEP provided an added value and that the extra time invested in his undergraduate program truly made a difference. Through his bilingual skills and his exposure to the world outside the U.S., he has become a competent cross-cultural communicator and global team player. He tells us also that he gained enormous confidence through his international education, and one result is his ability today to jump into projects which others avoid due to a fear of failure. Like so many IEP grads, John is

willing to take risks where major benefits could possibly accrue. As a result, he successfully took on two projects at his work in recent years that had been tried by others and dismissed as impossible.

4. *Think Big We Do.* Johnathan DiMuro certainly supports URI's right to promote itself with these words. And he certainly justifies the IEP's right to claim that it encourages "big thinking." If you want to be a chemical engineer, why not learn German along the way and spend a year expanding your perspectives through exposure to German higher education and industry? If you are doing well as an IEP student, why not submit yourself to the brutal application process and competition of the Truman Scholars Program? Then, if you want to explore public policy and sustainable development, why not apply to a prestigious program at Cambridge University? And, if you want to play a role in the evolution of a more sustainable chemical industry, why not seek a position with one of the giants in this field?

5. From John, as from our other graduates in this study, we learn the importance of the applied nature of language programming and instruction. John was an avid Spanish learner in school, but had assumed, before learning about the IEP, that language study and engineering study were mutually exclusive. The IEP enabled him not only to take language and culture courses, but to major in a language, spend a year abroad, and become a competent speaker and cross-cultural communicator. Language faculty across the country need to accept the simple fact that language learning can play a far greater role in the undergraduate curriculum if it integrates itself with other disciplines such as chemical engineering.

I will conclude this chapter on Johnathan DiMuro, just as will be done with each of the other case studies, with his definition of Global Engineer: *A global engineer interacts consistently with colleagues in other countries. I don't believe that it's necessary to live in a "foreign" country to be a global engineer. The challenges associated when interacting with colleagues on a global project over the phone and via email are often times greater than being outside your home country and the only one on the team who is non-native. Team dynamics with multiple cultures are difficult to manage, and the IEP prepared me to be aware and sensitive to issues that include but reach beyond language barriers.*

Eric McCoy Sargent

I can say with certainty that I would not be anywhere near where I am today, if not for the IEP. My experiences abroad shaped my career, absolutely, my life, definitely. I am more assertive and confident in my day-to-day activities because I feel like I've already achieved so much for my age. I am proud of myself for doing it.

Born: 1980
High School: Exeter/West Greenwich, Rhode Island
IEP Degrees: BA in German; BS in Mechanical Engineering, 2003
Graduate Degrees: University of Rhode Island, Masters of Science in Mechanical Engineering; Technische Universität Braunschweig, *Diplom-Ingenieur*
Current position: Senior Vehicle Engineer, BMW of North America
Past Position: Program Manager, ZF Lemforder Corp.
Personal: Married, one child

As a Senior Vehicle Engineer at BMW North America, Eric Sargent has what many young engineers would consider to be a dream job. Eric readily agrees while also pointing out that the job is not easy and getting there required an extraordinary effort. In this chapter we will look at Eric's life as a student and young engineer and explore how he reached his current position and what role the IEP played in his development.

Eric is a 2003 graduate of the IEP, having completed degrees in German and Mechanical Engineering. Following his undergraduate years, Eric entered the IEP Dual Degree Masters Program, and simultaneously earned the MS in mechanical engineering from URI and the masters-level *Diplom* from the Technical University of Braunschweig in Germany. In 2006 he was selected to join one of Germany's top automotive suppliers, ZF Friedrichshafen AG, by way of their fifteen-month International Post-Graduate Trainee Program. After the traineeship, he worked for three years with ZF in Friedrichshafen, Germany and Northville, Michigan before being recruited for a position at BMW of North America in 2010.

Eric works today as a bilingual, global engineer for BMW and is called upon for his technical expertise, his language skills, and his ability to function as a cross-cultural liaison. The BMW engineering team in Woodcliff Lake, New Jersey deals with all engineering issues emerging from the North American market in cooperation with the technical headquarters in Munich. What problems are Americans having with their BMW, MINI or Rolls-Royce vehicles? What needs are left unfulfilled by the current product? How can the BMW models be improved from the U.S. perspective? What are possible technical solutions for issues at hand?

Solving problems with German headquarters might seem like a very straight-forward task, requiring communication of very tangible matters by standard means, but it is far more complicated than simply reporting, for example, that a certain switch is defective or that the navigation system is not working up to a defined level of accuracy. In reality, this team of engineers treads daily on culturally complicated turf, often needing to remind the German lead engineers that their idea of driving is not necessarily equivalent to that of U.S drivers, or that market priorities in the U.S. are not necessarily what they are in Germany. A seemingly trivial example is the concept of the cup holder, which is crucial for Americans who have a far more relaxed driving style than do Germans and often sip coffee while behind the wheel. That such an amenity should be all-important is not readily apparent to the German engineers, for whom drinking coffee while driving is close to incomprehensible. It is issues such as this that made Eric so attractive for BMW of North America. There are, after all, very few American born engineers who speak German and have worked directly with German automotive engineers in Germany.

Eric tells us that while a fair amount of his work could be done by someone with less technical training than he has, his job could not be done by someone without fluency in the two languages and an understanding of the differences between the way Germans and Americans behave and function in their daily lives and without his understanding of the German engineering culture. At times he puts on his German hat to explain the Munich perspective to his American colleagues in New Jersey; at other times he wears his American hat, but uses his German cultural and linguistic knowledge, to help the Germans understand the background and importance of the U.S. needs. In addition to his extensive technical background and training, Eric is and must be a skilled cross-cultural communicator, dealing daily with both technical and linguistic/cultural matters.

Eric is an obvious success story who is frank about his indebtedness to the IEP, without which he would be following a very different career path today. Perhaps a closer look at Eric, his personality, his background, and his own goals might help us to understand why he is one of our "stars" today. Why did he opt for the IEP? Why did he become so fluent in German? What skills, interests or influences helped him to move from one step to the next?

Why was he a good candidate for international education, and why did he, in the long run, take it so seriously?

Eric is a modest and humble person, but at the same time clearly independent, confident, hard working and goal-oriented. If we follow our own stereotypical thinking, it would be easy to imagine Eric as the product of privilege, perhaps the son of an engineer, a high school honors student, a member of the track team, maybe even a valedictorian. Ironically, Eric was not a stellar student in high school and came very close to completely dropping out in his senior year. He does recall, however, that his fourth grade teacher identified him as an outstanding math student and told him that she would see his name in the paper someday because of his mathematical abilities. She wisely helped him gain confidence in the math and science areas and encouraged his inclinations in that direction. As a result, he was a good grade school student, and an honors student until his focus blurred in the tenth grade. The potential was always there, but in high school we probably would not have singled him out for success, based on standard judgment tools.

College was not automatic for Eric. There was not a strong push from home; his parents had not completed university degrees and his older brother had not gone to college. But a few things in high school played a role in helping him to see that a university education might be good for him. One was his French class trip to Paris in grade eleven, which gave him a glimpse into the larger world, and the second was a school visit from the URI assistant dean of engineering, whose enthusiasm for engineering and the IEP was contagious. Connecting engineering, technology, and especially cars with college, language, and international study and travel seemed to make a lot of sense to Eric at that time. Seeds were planted, even if they would not yet germinate.

Eric reports that his options for college were limited because of his lack of focus in high school and concomitant shaky record. Due to this and to his limited financial means, he applied for admission solely to URI which was located just a few miles from his home. He was fortunate to get a tip from his guidance counselor about a scholarship opportunity from the locally based GTech Corporation which he secured. Eric points out modestly the extent to which this was a lucky break, since he probably could not have afforded tuition otherwise.

When accepted at URI, based largely on his math and science grades and good SAT scores, he received more literature about the IEP in the mail and thought that might be a good option. Though he had studied French in high school, he opted for German at URI, since he thought this might possibly give him a chance to intern at his dream car company, BMW. At that point, the thought of studying another language was not exciting, but he could see the potential advantages. He tells us that he never really enjoyed the URI language classes, and found them to be his most difficult, even though he liked and respected the instructors. But he stuck with the program, motivated in part by the BMW idea, but also by the thought of going to Europe in his fourth year, seeing another part of the world and getting out of Rhode Island for a while. He clearly wanted to put some distance between himself and his high school years, and wanted to learn what was out there possibly waiting for him.

URI challenged Eric immediately and he responded with the gifts that his fourth grade teacher had identified. He not only did well academically, but also learned early and quickly to take advantage of opportunities that could open future doors and help with his financial situation. He interned for three summers in Rhode Island at GTech Corporation, a manufacturer of lottery systems. Though GTech would have been glad to have him stay on, things changed fast when he learned that the IEP had opened up summer internship opportunities with BMW Manufacturing Company in South Carolina. The program recommended him for an interview in South Carolina and Eric was able to intern at BMW the summer before his scheduled fourth-year academic year in Germany. This, in turn, helped make it possible for him to win an assignment at the Munich headquarters for his six-month German IEP internship. I was fortunate to be able to visit Eric at the internship site in South Carolina, a brand new plant where the BMW X5 (sport activity vehicle) and Z3 (roadster and coupe) were being manufactured for the world market. I will never forget seeing the proud look on Eric's face when I met him in the engineering offices of the plant, dressed in his BMW shirt, where he had been given real engineering assignments and was clearly performing to the satisfaction of his German boss, who is Eric's friend to this day.

Just as Eric had been on my doorstep when we first developed the possibility for internships at BMW in South Carolina and Munich, he also responded immediately when we opened the doors to the dual degree masters program with our partner university in Germany, the Technical University of Braunschweig. Having interned with German engineers in Munich, he learned not only that he needed a more in-depth engineering education to qualify as an engineer with such a group, but he also learned that they saw enough potential in him to suggest that he do his masters thesis in cooperation with them. Rather than go right into the workplace as an engineer, therefore, which he could have done, Eric decided to enter the new dual degree graduate program, leading simultaneously to the URI Masters of Science and the German *Diplom*, with a year at URI followed by a second year in Germany. Eric was willing and eager to do this, even though no one had done it yet, and he would clearly be a guinea pig. By this time, he clearly had his eyes set on the goal of a career in the automotive industry, with BMW as his first choice. The fact that there would be some bumps in the road with the new dual degree program did not bother him, such was the level of his risk taking skills in the name of an eventually more exciting career path.

With the help of his BMW mentor from South Carolina, Eric was able to intern at BMW in New Jersey for the summer between his graduation in 2003 and the first year of graduate school, at the location where he is now a Senior Vehicle Engineer. This in turn cemented his relationship with BMW even more, so that he would be able to do his thesis with the group at engineering headquarters in Munich. It also helped build his BMW network in general. His internship supervisor from that summer in New Jersey would also be his boss for his current position at BMW once he had his graduate degrees and a proven track record in the automobile industry.

The dual degree program was a sizeable challenge for Eric and for me as well, as I tried to help him steer his path through the maze of bureaucracy on both sides. It seems that any entrepreneurial step in academia is destined to be blocked by those who say we have never done it that way before and perhaps it simply cannot be done. But, he prevailed and the IEP prevailed, and with a rigorous year of graduate coursework at URI, additional courses, examinations, research projects and a thesis in Germany, Eric was able to graduate in 2006 with masters-level degrees from both URI and Braunschweig. In the United States he has a BS and MS in mechanical engineering and a BA in German. In Germany he is recognized prestigiously as a rare American with the title of *Diplom-Ingenieur* from the Technische Universität Braunschweig. The dual degree program not only gave him a greater depth of knowledge through his work at BMW and the Braunschweig Institute for Automotive Technology, it gave him the background and the credentials for full credibility with his colleagues in Germany.

Eric's thesis was complex, challenging, and unusual and illustrates the complexities of such a dual degree program. The dual masters requires one thesis, which is supervised and must be approved and accepted by faculty advisers at both institutions. In his case, he chose a topic to be done in conjunction with a BMW research team, which meant actually meeting the demands of three parties. In reality, however, there were four parties involved, since his research focused on the testing and validation of a complex GPS-based driving dynamics system that had been first developed by a team at Stanford University. Despite the hurdles and potential barriers, Eric dove into the project and completed it to the satisfaction of all parties. The latter was a learning process that took much more than technical skills; it also demanded personal tact, courage, political savvy, patience, and determination. Of course, these are all skills that are needed for a successful career in the global workplace.

Disappointingly, despite this superhuman effort, Eric was not able to land an appropriate position at BMW that summer, despite his unique qualifications. He did, however, participate successfully in a very competitive interview process for a management trainee program with another major player in the German automobile industry and another major partner for the IEP, ZF Friedrichshafen AG. The traineeship meant that he would have a full salary and an ongoing position with ZF, but that he would start first with a series of three projects providing exposure to different aspects of the company. The first position was in the Advanced R&D department in Friedrichshafen to develop software that would estimate vehicle dynamics using just a few sensors, in order to create a low-cost active suspension system for commercial freight vehicles. The second project was based in Northville, Michigan and was with the Corporate Logistics department. Eric functioned as "the German" responsible for visiting the North American facilities and implementing tools to better manage inventory and free up cash during the 2008 financial crisis. The third project was in Friedrichshafen in the Corporate Purchasing department, this time being the North American representative to learn the German system of supplier management, cost structure analysis and cost reduction. For this project he traveled to the main production facilities throughout Germany and to various suppliers to take part in cost reduction workshops.

Upon completion of the trainee program, Eric took a position with the North American headquarters of the company in Northville, Michigan. Though he could well have stayed on at the headquarters in Germany or landed with ZF in another country, he chose to come back to the U.S., where he did very well with ZF and advanced quite rapidly in the organization. He was given responsibilities in several areas, some more technical than others and some with a greater business orientation. He attributes his success at ZF to his very unusual background when compared with other engineers in the company. Being fluent in German and familiar with the R&D headquarters of the company in Germany, being able to interact between the two cultures, being able to exchange his German hat for his American hat gave him tremendous advantages over colleagues who were also technically savvy, but totally inexperienced in the cross-cultural realm. Eric was doing well with ZF and expected to be promoted again before too long.

Eric had naturally and wisely maintained his contacts with his former bosses and supervisors at BMW, knowing that BMW would someday have interest in a German speaking American engineer with experience in the automobile industry. Given the fact that ZF manufactures many components for BMW, such as the automatic transmissions and other driveline and chassis components, it is clear that Eric was well trained for their needs. Thus it is not surprising that his former internship supervisor at BMW North America was interested in having him back on board. Because he was doing well at ZF and indeed felt an obligation to them, Eric was reluctant to move. But the Senior Vehicle Engineer position at BMW was something he had wanted for a long time and it was an opportunity he couldn't pass up.

Eric is clearly the kind of graduate we hoped to have when we developed the IEP. He is bilingual, technically excellent, cross-culturally competent, and is comfortable with his role as a liaison between Munich and North America. Furthermore, he has achieved all of this by the age of thirty, and most certainly has a very promising future. While we take pride in the fact that the IEP helped Eric along the way, we need to ask what we as engineering, language and international educators can learn and in a sense take back from him for our future planning.

What can we learn from Eric Sargent?

1. Eric should first of all give us confidence in our belief that international education makes a difference. Certainly he would have been successful without the IEP. He could have continued his internships with GTech, for example, and possibly had a fine career there. But, the IEP experience gave him substantially new dimensions which he would not have had without learning German, studying and interning abroad, and finding his way to one of the world's leading car manufacturers. He himself tells us that he gained enormous personal confidence by working and studying in another culture and earning degrees that put him on a level playing field to work and/or compete with the best engineers in the world. Though these factors are scarcely to be measured, a simple look at his record is evidence enough to justify the title he gives himself on his resume: *global engineer*.

2. Eric should also expand our notions of who can learn a language, who should learn a language, how we can "sell" language learning to American students, and how students can have the best success at language learning. His case should also help us to dispel the myth that "English is enough." Though Eric tells us that language learning was not high on his list and that he would not have done it but for the opportunities provided by the IEP, he has indeed become fluent in the language. His self-described test for his ability in German is his ability to function in the language on a professional level. He reads German e-mails on a regular basis, communicates in German almost daily by phone, uses his German to convince the lead engineers in Munich of the BMW issues to be resolved for North America, and, perhaps, most notably, is proud to have survived many an uncomfortable situation at the bargaining table – in German.

    Eric's story teaches us that language learning needs to have direct applications if we wish to catch the attention of larger numbers of American students. It needs to be tied to other disciplines across the curriculum, engineering being one good example, and to future career opportunities. In short, it needs to intersect with students' lives. Though the basics can and must be supplied by the classroom at home, the learning process also needs to be reinforced through immersion experiences in the culture abroad. Eric would not have gained his language fluency without studying in Braunschweig and working at BMW in Germany, where he was forced to use the language as the primary means of communication.

3. The same can be said for study abroad. Who can do it? Who should do it? What are the parameters for a meaningful and valuable experience? And how do we win candidates for programs that meet the best criteria? Eric provides ample evidence that experiences abroad can be life changing and are extremely valuable in combination with rigorous study of any number of fields, with engineering being just one example. But, perhaps the debate today no longer needs to focus on whether study abroad is desirable, but the questions of how to do it, when to do it and for how long are still wide open. Many educators argue for any and all forms of study abroad, and we see widely diverse iterations from school to school. Would Eric have experienced his personal and professional growth if he had studied for a month or two in Finland, with all work done in English? Would it have been adequate to spend a summer doing project work with Chinese students in Beijing, again in English? Perhaps practicalities prohibit us from advocating that large numbers of students follow the model that Eric represents. Yet, if American universities do not make it possible for sizeable numbers to have in-depth experiences abroad, in the language, in the culture, then we as a

nation are not meeting the standards set by peer institutions and peer nations around the world.

4. Eric's story also underlines the importance of training young professionals to appreciate and deal with differences that are rooted in cultural tradition and perspective. He acquired cross-cultural communication skills through the materials that are integrated into the German language classes at URI and through the IEP pre-departure orientation, which helped open his eyes to the fact that Germans do in fact do it differently. Largely, however, this knowledge was acquired through the day-to-day experiences during his studies in Braunschweig and his internship and work experiences in Germany. Key to his success in this area is his ability to do it all in German. Without the language, he would not win the same respect from colleagues and superiors in Germany. Without the language, he would always be outside looking in.

5. On a more fundamental level, Eric should also cause us to reconsider the ways we decide who will be successful as a university student and what the main predictors are for both academic and professional success. It is important to note that family background, grades, attitude, high school performance and even social interaction were not predictors of success for Eric Sargent. He was a young man with tremendous potential, who needed a vision of something greater than his immediate surroundings to be able to unfold. We must do everything in our power to reach young students like Eric with challenging, yet exciting opportunities. It is not an exaggeration to say that the IEP was life-changing for Eric Sargent.

6. Eric's story also sends us a message about how we reach and recruit good students for our programs. Eric will never forget his fourth grade teacher who singled him out as an exceptional math student. Even though he did not catch fire until the university

level, he still had this moment of encouragement in the back of his mind. He also will always remember the day that the assistant dean of engineering from URI, Richard Vandeputte, came to his high school and shared his passion for engineering and the IEP. Without that visit he may well have followed through with his plans to simply drop out of high school at that time. The message for higher education is that high school outreach programs are extremely important. A visit to a high school may not seem important at the time and the immediate results may not be obvious. However, the seeds that are planted through a robotics team visit or the presentation by an assistant dean can easily be the necessary rescue of the kid in the back row who has lots of innate ability, but needs a push or helping hand from someone out there.

Eric Sargent made the following comments regarding characteristics of a global engineer: *Someone who can think and act internationally. More specifically, someone who recognizes the small details about getting business done by realizing that everyone is different and reacts differently given their background, and who can adapt their own work style to each situation.*

Ana Catalina Franco

Ana Franco at a Rugby game in Australia

My international experience during my undergrad years led to my first job which resulted in multiple projects and a trip to Germany to work with our counterparts. This in turn led me to gain global experience and establish greater credibility as I applied for an international program management role with my second employer.

Born: 1982 in Medellín, Colombia
Citizenship: USA
High School: Medellín, Colombia and Pawtucket, Rhode Island
Post High School: Community College of Rhode Island
IEP Degrees: BA in German; BS in Mechanical Engineering, 2006
Graduate Degree: University of Michigan, Masters of Science in Automotive Engineering
Current position: International Product Manager, Harris Corporation
Past Position: Product Development Engineer, DaimlerChrysler Corp., Auburn Hills, Michigan

Ana Franco, who graduated from URI in 2006 with degrees in Mechanical Engineering and German, is currently the international manager for a major product line of the Harris Corporation, a global supplier for defense, intelligence, and other assured communications needs. In this position she oversees projects in the millions of dollars, has responsibility for identifying and satisfying customer needs in multiple countries, assuring the highest quality of engineering and manufacturing, as well as preparing the company for the next steps in the product's development and market introduction. Having achieved this level of responsibility by the age of 29 is clearly no small feat. Ana deserves our attention.

Ana Franco at a defense systems trade show

Ana Catalina Franco is an American success story in the most classic and finest sense. Born, raised, and schooled

49

in Medellín, Colombia, she came to this country after she graduated from high school in Medellín in 1999, upon the strong encouragement of her parents and teachers. Her parents had divorced when she was a small child and her mother had emigrated to the U.S. at that time, pursuing better economic opportunities for herself and her daughter. Ana came with her mother when she was seven years old, but did not stay, opting to live with her father and extended family in Colombia. After graduating from high school with a good record, though, she decided to join her mother in Rhode Island and seek U.S. citizenship as well as a college education. She rightfully saw this as a wise next step, even though her immediate plan was to return home to Colombia after earning her U.S. college degree.

Knowing that her English was not strong enough, Ana spent her first year in Rhode Island taking classes at a high school in Pawtucket, getting a grasp on English and learning to understand how the system works in the U.S. for young people seeking higher education. After her high school year, she attended the Community College of Rhode Island where she improved her English drastically and demonstrated her abilities in math and science. With that success she was able to gain admission to URI through its very special Talent Development Program which advises and mentors disadvantaged students with academic potential. The TD program helped her secure a Pell grant and provided her with mentoring and a summer of university-level courses before her freshman year that would help ensure her success at URI.

Ana was ambitious and highly motivated to prepare herself for a productive life and career. She was encouraged by the fact that her mother had succeeded in the U.S., first as a nurses' assistant, then in business. Ana wanted to be the first in her family to earn a university degree, and thanks to her abilities in math and science, her goal would be to earn an engineering degree and to thereby hold a title which is so highly respected in Latin America.

Like many of her fellow students, Ana did not know about the IEP before coming to URI, but heard about it from another student and decided it would make sense to complete a Spanish degree along with her mechanical engineering degree. After her first Spanish course, however, she came to the conclusion that she could use her time better and open more doors for herself if she took on the challenge of a third language. By the next semester, therefore, she was enrolled in German classes, to be followed by URI's intensive summer immersion program, the German Summer School of the Atlantic, which enabled her to catch up to the level the program required by the end of her sophomore year.

Though many might have said that English and Spanish are enough, and that a recent Hispanic immigrant might better spend her time perfecting English rather than learning German, Ana believed, and proved to any doubters among us, that she could and would do it all. I clearly recall her visit to my office in the second semester of her freshman year, explaining that she wanted to do the German IEP. I told her she would be two semesters behind the students in her class in terms of German courses and would have to compensate through extra work at some point, most likely in our intensive summer program. I had my doubts about her taking on German, given the challenges of her engineering curriculum and other issues that relatively recent arrivees in the country might have to face. But for Ana the decision had been made; she knew that it would be worthwhile, and that she would follow through.

It is safe to say that Ana loved being an IEP student at URI and that the program and its associated infrastructure were helpful to her in several ways. Like most IEP students, she felt like she was part of a special group, and she intensified her relationship with other IEPers by living in the IEP House, the special residential facility for the program. Here she would be close to other students taking the same classes, finding it simple to join study groups, to be with students who valued her international background and goals, to discuss the future, and the best way to get there. As a recent immigrant, she no doubt felt some comfort in being part of a curriculum which valued other languages and cultures, Spanish included. Amazingly, her English was already so good at that point that most students were not aware that she had not grown up in the U.S. Ana confirms that it was special to be an IEP student at URI and that the program provided an atmosphere in which she could use her background, her native intelligence and determination to thrive.

Like Eric Sargent, Ana needed to earn money in the summer for school expenses, and wanted, therefore, to find paying internships. She achieved this for the summer after her sophomore year by attending the annual conference of the Society of Hispanic Professional Engineers (SHPE), an organization she had been active in at URI, where she caught the attention of recruiters from Kimberly-Clark and secured her 2003 summer engineering internship in Wisconsin. By the next summer (2004) she was able to find an internship through SHPE with DaimlerChrysler in Detroit and gain experience in her preferred automotive area with a German-American company. Very much like the Eric Sargent model, she was able to intern with this North American branch of a global car manufacturer in anticipation of doing her six-month German internship the following year with the German headquarters of the same company, in this case at the Mercedes R&D center.

Ana spent the 2004-2005 academic year in Germany, studying for the fall semester at the Technical University of Braunschweig and then doing her internship at Mercedes (DaimlerChrysler) in Sindelfingen with a focus on steering and handling research. While in Braunschweig, she worked to improve her German, got her first exposure to German culture, and also took courses in that school's Institute for Automotive Technology. The latter helped her gain the technical vocabulary and exposure to scientific texts which she would put to good use during her internship with Mercedes R&D engineering headquarters.

During her final year at URI (fifth year IEP students refer to themselves as super seniors) Ana once again made good use of the opportunities afforded by the IEP and interviewed with several companies. She also opted to take advantage of the first IEP intensive six-week summer course in Chinese which was held at Zhejiang University in Hangzhou immediately after graduation. Wisely she decided to delay entry to the workforce by these six-weeks in order to begin learning Mandarin and to gain exposure to the Chinese culture.

Ana had learned about the Chrysler Institute of Engineering (CIE) while doing her internship in Detroit in the summer before going to Germany and had remained in contact with its administrators since that time. Not surprisingly the CIE also stayed in touch with her. With Ana's internship experiences with the company in both the U.S. and Germany, her fluency in German, English, and Spanish, her excellent academic record, and her clear eagerness and ability to go the extra mile, she was identified as a superior candidate for the CIE's Management Development Program. She thus spent her first two career years with Daimler-Chrysler rotating through business, manufacturing, and technical departments at Chrysler headquarters in Auburn Hills, Michigan and simultaneously completing a company sponsored MS program in automotive engineering at the University of Michigan.

Had the DaimlerChrysler merger been a success, Ana no doubt would have remained and advanced with that organization. Her talent and background was valued there and she participated in several collaborative projects with engineers in Germany and was sent to Germany to spearhead cross-functional collaboration for the Chassis Department. When the company broke up shortly after that trip, however, with Daimler pulling out, the immediacy of her German background was sadly no longer of great interest to her superiors. And when things turned sour for Chrysler with the economic downturn, the company felt compelled to eliminate 25% of its workforce, even though that would mean losing most of its younger employees and almost all of the CIE recruits. Ana decided that her professional growth would have better prospects in another setting and left Chrysler voluntarily, even if not eagerly, when a buy-out incentive was offered to all engineers. As a footnote, it is well worth mentioning that her departure from Chrysler which had less apparent need for skills facilitating global collaboration is more than ironic. Chrysler today is owned largely by Fiat! Had that been on the table at the time of the buyout and had her bosses known that Ana also had studied Italian in her last year at URI, they may have been more reluctant to let her leave.

The DaimlerChrysler failure was a clear disappointment for Ana who was poised to play a key role as an intermediary and leader for cross-functional collaboration. Looking back, however, she does not regret the turn of events, since it did enable her to launch her career as a global engineer who would be able to find appropriate work to continue that path.

After Chrysler, Ana looked for a position with a global company that would appreciate her technical education through the masters level, her business training and experience, her international experience, and her cross-cultural communication skills. This she found in the Harris Corporation, a communications company with over 16,000 employees, which serves government and commercial needs in the markets of 150 countries. Parallel to Daimler-Chrysler, Harris recognized Ana's manifold skills and rich background, and offered her a position starting with their twelve-month Management Development Rotational Program. Here she would gain exposure to Department of Defense product management, international product management, international sales, growth initiatives, and various supporting departments on the business, manufacturing, and research and development sides. As Ana explains, the point of the program was to develop the proper network and expertise required to land a position in one of the Harris main business units, i.e., to help promising employees transition from the "back-end of the business to the front-end of the business." In her case the focus was largely international due to her special set of qualifications in that area.

Harris obviously recognizes that Ana is a very motivated, driven, ambitious and talented young woman.

They also equally appreciate and value the depth of her international experience. Though she currently is not regularly called upon to use her language skills, she is respected for her trilingualism, and valued for her ability to work comfortably and ably with customers from other national and cultural settings. Shortly after completing the management trainee program she was, therefore, appointed international manager for a key product line of the company. As is the case with Eric Sargent in his current position, the technical education and training is an absolute must for this position, but equally important is the ability to apply that knowledge in many different cultural settings. Without the IEP, without her Hispanic background, without her work at a German university and in the R&D center of Mercedes, Ana would not have been offered her current position.

As an International Product Line Manager (PLM) Ana manages the development, engineering, manufacturing, marketing and sales of a specific line of radios sold mainly for military installations. In this role, she directs graphic designers to create the marketing material for her needs, she works with a global sales team to brief and sell her product appropriately and works with engineering and manufacturing to make sure the product is built to the highest quality. Ana tells us that the most important aspect of her job is interacting with end customers in order to properly translate desires and needs into product requirements at the Harris facilities. Since Harris has customers in over 130 countries, she must travel quite a bit and has travelled since her recent appointment to Australia, Abu Dhabi, Egypt, Dubai and Brazil. Though she has not travelled yet to Germany or Latin America, she has received potential customers who appreciated her presentations in Spanish. She also recently pleased a key customer from Germany whom she greeted and conversed with in German when he visited the headquarters in Rochester, much to his surprise. Not surprisingly, Ana is now learning Portuguese on her own to be able to interact better with her customers from Brazil.

Cross-cultural communication is key to Ana's

success in her position. Every day she is dealing with customers or members of her sales team, who are currently dispersed across approximately thirty different countries. In dealing with customers or Harris colleagues in Latin America, Europe, Asia or the Middle East, she needs to be alert to their needs and their cultural perspectives. When going to the Middle East, for example, she has to be able to compensate for the fact that women and/or young persons such as herself are typically not in her kind of position. When dealing with Chinese versus Germans or Mexicans, she needs to be mindful of differences in communication style. This applies to e-mails, to video-conferences, to personal visits, to contracts, and the myriad of details associated with the products she represents.

Ana goes the extra mile in several ways. Here as an avid triathlon competitor.

What can we in higher education learn from Ana?
    1. As was the case with others, it is clear that Ana would have been successful in her engineering career with or

without the IEP. She is bright, motivated, a positive and pleasant person, all features pointing to success in the traditional monocultural mode of the past, and there are ample numbers of companies which do not specifically look for international and cross-cultural expertise. On the other hand, it is also clear that the IEP opened the doors for the opportunities afforded her by DaimlerChrysler and the Harris Corporation. By being a risk taker, by going the extra mile, by always taking her work to the challenge level, and by preparing herself to work globally, Ana caught the attention of the recruiters in search of candidates for their leadership track positions and in search of candidates who could meet their needs in the global environment. The IEP, with its second degree and its full year of study and internship abroad helped to set her apart, to provide her with special and unique qualifications to meet the needs of world-class companies for which global preparation has become more the norm than the exception. Ana's case provides clear evidence that a thorough-going international education for engineers such as that offered by the IEP makes a significant difference; it provides qualifications which are increasingly in demand and opens the doors to leadership track positions.

2. Ana's case also sends a message regarding opportunities that should be provided for students who come to us as recent immigrants or as the offspring of immigrant families. Hispanic Americans, Asian Americans and others who come to the university with bilingual and cross-cultural knowledge and experience are rarely told by their families, their teachers or their universities that their languages other than English are an asset to be treasured, refined, and maintained. Likewise, it is rarely pointed out to students like Ana that they have the chance during their undergraduate years to acquire a third language and build upon their already

existing global skills to take themselves to a level which is common among their peers from other countries but rare among U.S. Americans. Universities should be getting this message out in the schools to the children of immigrant or recent immigrant families. They need to learn early on that their Spanish, Chinese, Korean, Russian or other language skills are an important asset to be nurtured rather than overcome.

3. Ana Franco's path to success began with educational experiences at the Community College of Rhode Island and was then jump started at the university level with the assistance of URI's Talent Development Program and a Pell Grant. Had these opportunities not been there to help her with her English and allow her to demonstrate her talent in the areas of mathematics and science, she may never have made it to a college degree. We need to continually remind ourselves that immigrants coming to the country often have enormous talent hidden behind cultural and linguistic barriers. It is in our national interest to provide every opportunity for new citizens to succeed.

4. Ana also sends a message regarding the appropriateness of language learning for engineers and, in her case, for engineering students who are immigrants. Though she had at first thought of the IEP as an opportunity to complete a Spanish major, it was her own determination and courage that led her to the decision to learn German, even when she herself felt she was still learning English. In her case, language learning has become second nature and she tells us that the process has become part of her being, making it easier with each new language. Though fluent "just" in English, Spanish, and German, she also has taken Italian courses and upon graduation she took a six-week intensive Mandarin course in China before beginning her job with DaimlerChrysler. As noted with Ana and other

58

similar cases, bilingualism or trilingualism is fully attainable and it is our role in higher education to provide the framework and opportunities to make it doable. Given the chance and the clarity of the reason for doing so, students will respond.

5. Ana's case also has a message for us regarding study abroad. We might think that recent immigrants should focus on adjustment to life in the U. S. or that there is no need to study abroad if a student is already bilingual and already lived a significant portion of his or her life another country. We have learned in the IEP, however, that students coming to us from other countries, whether as immigrants or foreign students should be equally encouraged to take on a third language, a third culture, and should be equally encouraged to study abroad, even if already on a study-abroad platform in the U.S. Other URI examples include a young woman from Japan who did the German IEP as a foreign student at URI and now works for a German company in Tokyo. We likewise currently have a student from China who is spending this academic year as a German IEP student in Germany. Last year a Nigerian student completed the German IEP as well, having studied in Braunschweig and completed an internship with Siemens AG.

As with the other alums in this volume, I will conclude the chapter on Ana Franco with her definition of a global engineer as a professional: *who is keen to respond to cultural sensitivities and is able to build the business acumen required for today's global workforce. He or she not only understands highly complex technical problems, but also understands today's complex global dynamics. What happens in Japan, Libya, Egypt or any other country today can affect how we do business in the U.S. tomorrow.*

Jesse Michael Schneider

The IEP offered - hands down - the best possibility in the U.S to become a bilingual, truly international engineer. I was always motivated to work in the international automotive industry and the IEP offered a once in a lifetime, competitive advantage to achieve this goal.

Born: 1971
High School: Cranston, Rhode Island
IEP Degrees: Bachelor of Science in Mechanical Engineering, 1994; Intensive language study at URI's German Summer School of the Atlantic and Germany's Goethe Institute (1994)

Current position: Manager of Requirements for "Clean Energy Systems" Department at BMW AG in Munich, Germany.

Past Positions: Head of Research and Development at Proton Motor Fuel Cells, Munich, Germany; Hybrid Vehicle Concepts Manager at Chrysler Corporation, Michigan; Manager of Fuel Cell Vehicle Safety, Codes and Standards, and Hydrogen Infrastructure for DaimlerChrysler (Mercedes Division); Senior Engineer, Fuel Cell Vehicle Program, DaimlerChrysler (Mercedes Division); Product Engineer in Fuels & Exhaust Systems, DaimlerChrysler; Process Engineer Exhaust Systems, Zeuna Stärker (Currently Faurecia); Test Engineer, ZF Friedrichshafen AG, Friedrichshafen, Germany

Personal: Married, one child. Dual Citizenship: U.S., Italian

Jesse Schneider had always been an avid car buff and eager to launch a career in the automotive industry. He also was very interested in environmental causes, which would later help shape his career. When he noted in his senior year at URI that Ford was launching its first global car, the Mondeo, he realized that automobile manufacturing had become a global business and that his chances of making it in this field would be greatly enhanced with global skills, e.g., with languages and international experience. But he was already a senior in mechanical engineering and not an IEP student. *What could he do?*

How well I remember him coming to my office, regretting that he had not joined the IEP as a freshman, and asking if there were not some way to compensate for what he now saw as a foolish mistake. Believing that it is never too late for a convert to the IEP, I laid out a plan for Jesse that would mean delaying entry to the workforce, but would open doors for him not otherwise available. I suggested that he start taking German during his last semester at URI, continue in the summer at URI's immersion program, the German Summer School of the Atlantic, and then enroll in two consecutive intensive courses at the Goethe Institute in

Germany. I promised Jesse that I would have an internship lined up for him in the German automobile industry at the conclusion of the second Goethe Institute course, assuming he was successful with his German language learning.

Jesse proved that he was more than serious about pursuing this path and more than willing to make the necessary sacrifice. In short, he followed my proposal exactly and with great success. I did my best to support him by finding scholarship aid at the Goethe Institute and standing by with advice. The pace of his German learning was almost brutal, but he stuck with it, and has never regretted his decision to accept the challenge that would not only open the doors to a career in the global automobile industry, but would impact his personal life as well. In 1994, during his first few months in Germany, Jesse met and fell in love with a young Italian graduate student, who was taking additional classes at the Goethe Institute in Iserlohn, Germany. Her name is Laura and she has been Jesse's wife for the past 13 years and is the mother of their daughter, Miriam. The relationship with Laura and her family meant branching out to yet another language and culture; Jesse has in the meantime become a fluent speaker of Italian as well as German, and he recently acquired his Italian citizenship.

Following Jesse's second Goethe Institute course, he interned in Germany at the R&D headquarters of ZF Friedrichshafen AG, one of the IEP's major corporate partners and sponsors. There he was given the task of validating a new dynamic pressure measuring system for gaskets in a running transmission, a task that he carried out so well that they hired him on contract for another six months as a test engineer, as he had already had his engineering degree. This meant that Jesse would have a full year's experience working with German engineers in a highly respected company and also that his language skills would be very strong along with his understanding of life in Germany and its cultural differences.

Jesse's background at this point was distinguished by his accomplishments in engineering, his fluency in German, and his cross-cultural communication skills, all of which led

62

him to a salaried job with Zeuna Stärker (Faurecia today) Exhaust Systems in Augsburg, Germany, a company which had won the contract for the exhaust systems for the BMW sports car, the Z3, which was to be produced in Spartanburg, South Carolina. Jesse began his work for them in Germany, for a one year, rotational trainee-program. He would be trained for the Z3 exhaust production and then sent to South Carolina as the sole American engineer in the U.S. branch of the company with German language fluency and extensive experience in the German headquarters.

With two years of experience in the German-American automobile industry under his belt, Jesse found that his resume was of interest on a broader basis and began to receive offers, especially after the merger of Daimler and Chrysler. In 1998, he and Laura moved to Detroit, where Jesse worked as an exhaust system product release engineer for the Dodge Durango and Dodge Ram sport utility vehicles. Given his skill in working with both German and American engineers, he initiated a synergy effort on exhaust catalytic converters, internally at the Chrysler Group and in the Mercedes group which ended up saving the company 100's of millions of dollars and is still used to this day. He then rotated as the product release engineer for the diesel fuel systems of the Cummins engines, where he successfully launched the exhaust systems and Chrysler's first CDI Diesel Fuel System into production.

Jesse's career took on an exciting twist for a young engineer when he approached a Mercedes Manager, Christian Mohrdieck (now director of Mercedes fuel cell program), and asked him if they needed a "fuels engineer for fuel cell vehicles" at the fuel cell program office in Stuttgart, Germany. He explained his personal and professional goal to "take the automobile from the carbon equation."

Not long after that he received a surprise call from the Mercedes Benz Research, Engineering, Design office (REDNA) out of Palo Alto, California. He was asked to join the Mercedes Group at DaimlerChrysler who were committed to the development of the very forward-looking and highly experimental fuel cell technology. Jesse was soon sent to Sacramento for a three-year assignment at the Mercedes office within the newly formed California Fuel Cell Partnership (CaFCP). There he would represent Daimler-Chrysler's contribution to this consortium of eight automobile manufacturers, five oil companies, hydrogen fueling suppliers, and the U.S. and California governments. Jesse made a name for himself in this field. As Senior Engineer Fuel Cell Project he carried out vehicle testing, benchmarking, and change management for Mercedes USA and was responsible for four generations of fuel cell vehicle change management and also developed a methanol onboard storage system for a methanol fuel cell vehicle.

There, Jesse led a number of worldwide firsts for fuel cell vehicles, including: the Emergency Responder Guide for CaFCP, hydrogen quality guidelines, hydrogen fueling guidelines and a station test apparatus. In 2002, at Mercedes, he conceptualized, organized and implemented the first fuel cell vehicle coast-to-coast trip in the U.S. Until 2011, it was the longest continuous public road drive for any fuel cell vehicle. From 2004-2006 he was manager for the DaimlerChrysler fuel cell fleet safety, coordinator for U.S. hydrogen infrastructure, and for U.S. hydrogen and fuel cell vehicle codes and standards. He has also led development of the first worldwide fuel cell standards and fueling guideline standards for the Society of Automotive Engineers (SAE). And he has been nominated as the sole consultant for the U.S. Department of Energy Hydrogen Safety Panel, and the sole representative for the U.S. automotive industry on the topic.

Jesse is the first to point out that these career steps would not have happened were it not for the IEP. Strong engineering skills were a given for these tasks, but he would not have been considered without his German experience, and, above all, his ability to meet the German project leaders on their own linguistic and cultural turf. As Jesse puts it in his own words: *The IEP made it possible to work in the German automotive industry, where knowing the language and understanding the culture is essential in communication. Even though every German engineer knows a high level of English, they do not use it internally when discussing technical projects and objectives.*

Unfortunately, it says a great deal about American values and short-sightedness that Jesse's accomplishments and skills in this important new area of research and development were not utilized after Daimler pulled out of the partnership with Chrysler. He stayed on after the de-merger as a manager of the Chrysler Hybrid Vehicle Concepts Department, but no longer found himself involved with fuel cell technology and no longer found himself valued for his global skill set. It is quite ironic, as was the case for Ana Franco, that he left given that Chrysler is now one-third owned by Fiat and Jesse is fluent in Italian as well as German, not to mention his citizenship!!

Jesse, after 10 years of combined Daimler and Chrysler, took the buyout-package and set out to find something different. Coincidentally, a headhunter representing a small fuel cell systems company in Munich, Germany contacted him about a job interview. With a German-speaking Italian wife and a mutual desire to raise their daughter internationally and multi-lingually, a move back to Germany would not be a problem, indeed it would be welcome. In 2009, therefore, Jesse took a position as Head of Research and Technology for Proton Motor Fuel Cells in Puchheim, Germany (near Munich) where he would lead four departments related to fuel cell technology and also create a fuel cell program for extending the range of commercial electric vehicles.

Parallel to his positions at DaimlerChrysler and later Proton Motor, he chaired a number of SAE Standard committees on a number of world first standards: SAE J2799, 70MPa (10,000Psi) Hydrogen Fueling Nozzle & Vehicle-Station Communications (2007); SAE J2601, Hydrogen Fueling Guideline (2010, only standard of its kind worldwide); SAE J2954, Wireless Charging of Electric and Hybrid Electric Vehicles (draft).

Since there was no organized activity in Munich on Hydrogen, but many of the key companies were there (Linde, BMW, LBST, TÜV Süd, Energy Technologies, and others), he initiated the "Bavarian Hydrogen Stammtisch." Since 2009, it is a "grass-roots" roundtable to discuss fuel cell coordination activities in Bavaria. (For those unfamiliar with the concept of "Stammtisch," such is a regular meeting place and time for a few evening beers, where the problems of the world are solved. The Stammtisch is in reality a very important cultural concept, especially in the South.)

At the end of 2010, at this "Stammtisch," over a good Bavarian beer, Jesse was approached by the head of the BMW Hydrogen Program, Tobias Brunner, and asked if he would like to help start an effort there in fuel cell vehicles and continue his efforts in the wireless charging of electric vehicles.

Since 2011, therefore, he has been the manager responsible for the specifications, standardization, and testing of both hydrogen fuel cell drive trains and wireless charging systems at the BMW Technology and Innovation Center in Munich. This entails designing specifications of alternative propulsion and the storage for hydrogen fuel cell systems, which is one of the major stumbling blocks for this technology. Wireless charging of electric vehicles is also on Jesse's list, letting us know that the long-awaited "plug-in" vehicle technology in this country is already passé. Head of "CryoCode", German Government and Industry Project, Testing Program for validating cryo-compressed (high density hydrogen storage) hydrogen storage for future standardization.

What can we as engineering, language, and international educators learn from Jesse Schneider?
1. The very first lesson learned in his case is that it is "never too late," even though we remain with "the sooner the better" as a guiding principle. The IEP is based upon an integrated curriculum that begins on day-one of the freshman year and there is ample reason for that. But we should not dismiss the possibility that missed opportunity can be made up with alternative tracks, in this case one that may be characterized as the "Jesse Schneider express route."

The IEP is carefully planned and structured for the dual degree outcome (BS/BA), where Jesse had received a B.S. in engineering, but the second degree here is not necessarily the absolute or most important outcome. What was critical for Jesse as a graduate engineer with the goal of working with the German automobile industry was gaining fluency in German and an ability to work efficiently and smoothly with global teams. This does not mean backing off from high standards, but rather an openness to achieving the goal through different sequences. While maintaining our standards, therefore, we must be willing to bend our program to fit the individual,

2. We learn from Jesse that it is hardly harmful to take extra preparation time beyond the classic four-year college education. While Jesse could certainly have found an engineering job upon graduation in 1994, he decided to spend a year learning German and doing an internship with a company in Germany. As is the case with other IEP students, he most definitely would have succeeded in a traditional way without the IEP, and that may well have been the preferred path from the point of view of parents and friends, but his success as we know it today would not have been possible without the extra time. Was it worth it? That requires a judgment call on each of our parts. But we know what Jesse's answer is.

3. Along with the other IEP alums working globally, Jesse sends the message loud and clear that, though English is the world language, it is not enough in the global R&D workplace. As true as it may be that the German fuel cell technology team in Stuttgart can speak English, it is not their preferred working language or their language of daily practice. At international conferences they give their papers in English, and they read the literature on their specialty published in English, but they do their best work, their thinking, their dreaming, their problem solving and decision making in their native tongue.

Jesse needed to be respected as an engineer to enter their group, and for this he needed to be able to do it on their turf, and in their language. Without his global skills, his current career focused on expertise in an extremely important area of research and development on behalf of one of the world's most respected automobile companies (BMW AG) would not have been possible. Jesse's career path leads us to ask how much we are missing as Americans as a result of our neglect of serious foreign language education, a question that becomes more and more critical as research and development in so many areas is increasingly in the hands of scientists and engineers abroad.

4. Jesse gives us bragging rights to just about all of our claims as international educators. Learning a language opens doors, removes barriers, and creates new opportunities. Studying abroad is a life changing experience. In his case, it not only gave access to a very special career, but it led to his lifelong partnership with his wife Laura, the birth of their daughter Miriam, and for Jesse even a dual citizenship shared with his wife and daughter.

5. As is the case for so many IEP grads, Jesse tells us that it is the language skills that provide the competitive advantage when seeking engineering positions in the global workplace. He reports that he would not have been offered his last five jobs without his fluency in German. And once again it is the connection of language learning with the professional field that makes this magic happen. Jesse did not sacrifice a year to learn German solely out of love for language learning. He did so to enhance his career options in the global automobile industry. Learning Italian also had a direct application and clarity of motivation. Italian would give him greater insight into the culture of his wife and a closer relationship with her and her family. It is not

surprising that Jesse, now that he speaks Italian well, has also received job offers in Italy.

6. As we will see in the case of Chris and Mike Smith, global education, along with its many benefits, provided strength to the backbone of Jesse's and Laura's marriage. They met as two foreigners learning German in Germany, one from Italy, one from the United States. Together they have lived in Germany and in the United States, and spent considerable time in Italy. They share three cultures and three languages with each other and with their daughter, and he enjoys an Italian citizenship along side his American citizenship. They are proudly an international couple, mobile, flexible, tolerant, able to pursue their own interests as a couple in concert with his professional path.

For Jesse Schneider: *To be a global engineer, you need first to have the capacity to listen, learn and implement. Even though you can learn a language, understanding the differences in culture, sometimes major, are also a key in working with people in a foreign country. In the automotive business, it is very important to be able to arrive at the milestones which are not always easy to meet. The expectations are higher than in almost any other industry. Failure is not an option.*

A global engineer is able to work in an international environment and able to meet the expectations of these projects inside a multi-cultural setting. Sometimes it means travel to different countries where English may or may not be common. Either way, a global engineer has the ability to take his/her skill set and adapt it to a dynamic work environment to "get the job done."

Sonia Gaitan

Sonia (right) with a colleague at Johnson & Johnson

Born: Valledupar, Colombia
Citizenship: USA
Age: 28
High Schools: Valledupar, Colombia and Central Falls, Rhode Island
IEP Degrees: BA in Spanish (with Portuguese); BS in Chemical Engineering, 2005
Graduate Degrees: Planning an MBA on Supply Chain Management
Current position: Senior Supply Chain Network Planner for McNeil Consumer Healthcare, the largest consumer company within the Johnson & Johnson Family of Companies
Past Positions: Quality Engineer I, Quality Engineer II, Senior Quality Assurance Engineer, Johnson & Johnson

With IEP, you immerse yourself in another culture and develop critical "soft" skills. I work confidently with business partners from all parts of the world and all walks of life and achieve results. I can adapt quickly to changing environments and situations.

Sonia mentoring future global engineers

Sonia Gaitan is the second Hispanic alumna partici-pating in this study and she too depicts the IEP as a key part of her path to the American Dream. Hers is a story of parents determined to come to a country where their three daughters could have a university education with far better chances for employment, professional advancement, and stable livelihoods. At the start of this study Sonia was a Senior Quality Assurance Engineer at Johnson & Johnson global headquarters in New Jersey. Since that time, she has advanced to Senior Supply Chain Network Planner for McNeil Consumer Healthcare, the largest consumer company within the Johnson & Johnson family of com-panies. With such major professional achievement in a short period of time, Sonia has indeed made her and her parents' dream a reality.

Sonia came from Colombia at the age of six when she and her family settled with relatives in Central Falls, Rhode Island, a predominantly immigrant city with a reputation for poverty, unemployment, and a very troubled school system. Despite the odds, her parents were determined to achieve their goals and to do whatever might be necessary to give their children a sound education. When her mother feared for the negative social influences surrounding Sonia as a freshman in high school, she took her back to Colombia and enrolled her in an intensive science and math track in the high school there for the next two years. This was a huge step, but her mother thought it was necessary for Sonia to overcome the negativism that pervades so much of the U.S. school system, especially in downtrodden areas like Central Falls, and to gain an appreciation for what life in the U.S. could offer. Sonia returned to Central Falls for her senior year, did very well, received her diploma and qualified to study engineering at URI.

As was the case for Ana Franco, Sonia gained acceptance to URI through the special Talent Development Program which identifies and mentors promising students from disadvantaged environments. TD advised Sonia, helped her secure a Pell Grant, and gave her a head start with tutoring and introductory summer courses before the fall semester of her freshman year. Sonia had learned about the IEP through a student presentation at her high school in her senior year and was ecstatic to discover a program which identified her native language and Latin American cultural background as an asset for her future rather than a past to be overcome. Fortunately the IEP and Talent Development are compatible and had formed a mutually supportive relationship to help and support students like Sonia.

Working toward a degree in Spanish along with chemical engineering was a good choice for Sonia, even though Spanish was her first language. The program enabled her to improve her literacy skills in Spanish, including technical writing, and to study the literatures and cultures of the broader Spanish-speaking world. She also was able to take advantage of a special track for native or near-native speakers of Spanish which included the study of Portuguese.

Sonia took full advantage of the IEP. As a resident of the IEP House, she was able to bond with other students from similar backgrounds, with students taking the same courses and preparing for parallel futures, and with students who valued her language skills. In the IEP House, she could both tutor and be tutored, she could have easy access to the IEP staff and faculty, and she could enjoy an environment which valued and nurtured good study habits. Here she could feel at home and secure in the otherwise sometimes intimidating environment of a state university campus. Before coming to the university, Sonia did not know the reality of being part of a minority group, as her exposure to the world had been limited mainly to Central Falls, Rhode Island and Colombia.

When it came time for her year abroad, Sonia wisely branched out for experiences outside of the worlds she already knew. As a result she spent her 2003 fall semester studying engineering at the Centro Politecnico de Zaragoza in Spain, and the following six months completing an internship at a Johnson & Johnson plant in Sao Paulo, Brazil. Her experience in Spain was valuable, even if a bit disappointing at the time. Arriving at the beginning of the Iraq war, she found herself surrounded by a wave of anti-Americanism, which was more intense for her, since she also experienced a degree of prejudice toward Latin Americans. Her best memories in Spain are related to time spent in the larger metropolitan areas of Madrid and Barcelona, where she found people far more open, tolerant and worldly.

Sonia established initial contact for her internship with Johnson & Johnson through her own initiative. As was the case for Ana Franco, Sonia was active in the URI chapter of the Society for Professional Hispanic Engineers (SHPE) and approached J&J at the organization's annual conference, where she was hired as a summer intern with the

J&J Consumer Division in New Jersey. As a result of this initiative and her success as an intern, the company chose to familiarize itself with URI and the IEP, and agreed that the idea of a six-month internship for Sonia in Brazil would be an excellent idea, both for her and the company. She could gain first-hand exposure to the company, to the Brazilian culture, and refine her speaking ability in Portuguese, and possibly become a valuable candidate for a future full-time position. This would be the first internship placement for the IEP in Brazil, and it was the first time for Johnson & Johnson to make such an arrangement. The effort was not easy at the time, but it succeeded and proved to be very worthwhile.

Sonia was immediately given major responsibilities as an intern in Sao Paulo, where she worked with a "formulator team," which was charged with defining concepts for new products and bringing them from the idea level to actual production within a short time period. This involved formulating the product for potential markets in Latin and North America, conducting consumer studies, creating specifications and running pilots. Sonia learned a great deal in this position, performed well and made many friends along the way.

Sonia's work with Johnson & Johnson in Brazil was recognized by her immediate bosses who transferred that information to Todd Allen, the IEP's recruiter contact at the New Jersey-based company, who in turn followed Sonia through her final year at URI and then extended an offer as a first-step Quality Assurance Engineer at the corporate headquarters.

Sonia still maintains contacts with the plant in Sao Paulo, especially as she is the only engineer in New Jersey who speaks Portuguese. As a Senior Quality Assurance Engineer her responsibilities have been global, extending far beyond one location abroad. Sonia has been part of a team of engineers who must guarantee the quality for all of the Johnson & Johnson baby products worldwide. This is a huge and very well-known product line for the company, worth billions in annual sales, and which are the result of global collaboration, with products or ingredients of products originating from J&J facilities and/or sub-contractors across the United States and the entire world. Responsibility for the quality of these products wherever they might be sold is a huge undertaking.

Global engineering for Sonia has meant working with engineers at Johnson & Johnson locations in Latin America (Colombia, Mexico, the Dominican Republic, Puerto Rico, Brazil), Italy, France, Australia, China, Georgia, Tennessee, Michigan, just to name a few states or countries. She is often called upon to conduct extensive quality assurance visits at these locations or to participate in the leadership of teams communicating remotely. As the global headquarters, New Jersey sets the standards for quality and must be sure that compliance is 100%.

Sonia is grateful to the IEP for her cross-cultural and language training which is put to use on a daily basis. One can only imagine the sensitivity needed to work with clients from China to Mexico, especially as the person who has the power to close a facility down. In her words: "The IEP prepared me to deal with diverse work environments and personally taught me not to judge a book by its cover. You need to understand the difference in the culture you're dealing with in order to communicate efficiently." Sonia has learned that " the relationship is crucial to obtaining optimal results with international affiliates" and that language plays a key role. She is grateful for the language skills she has and uses them regularly, while also being motivated to learn Italian and French.

To cite some specific examples of her global interaction, Sonia was sent recently to a J&J facility in Colombia to conduct a week-long microbiology-based training seminar on the standards and best practices for cleaning and sanitation related to production. As a native speaker, it was, of course, to her advantage to conduct the sessions entirely in Spanish, which was greatly appreciated by the participants. Recently she was on the phone in Spanish to engineers in Puerto Rico and the Dominican Republic and in Portuguese with colleagues in Sao Paulo.

75

Like many other IEP grads working with global teams, she is also regularly part of telecommunications meetings with engineers from countries such as China, Australia, Mexico, and Brazil, which require her to be working very early in the morning or late in the evening.

In reflecting on the impact of the IEP on her life and career, Sonia believes that she is a better engineer, not necessarily in a purely technical sense, but in the sense that she has a greater appreciation for the perspectives of others, is more creative in solving problems, and in communicating such solutions. She feels that the IEP, by teaching her to be more open-minded and accepting of difference, made her a better person.

When asked about outside interests and hobbies, it is very telling that Sonia spoke first of her commitment to giving back what she has learned by reaching out to high school students living in environments similar to that of her own teenage years. Each month she volunteers at a local high school in New Jersey where the majority of students are Latino or Black and where there is a high rate of poverty and social stress. She understands the negative attitudes that prevail and tries to help the students understand that attending school, learning, studying, and striving for a middle class future can be cool, contrary to what so many are feeling or are made to feel. *I meet with high-risk students and try to motivate them to stay in school. I come from their same background, as an immigrant, and grew up in a bad neighborhood. I show them that it's possible to make it and to achieve success through school.*

Given the success of IEP alums like Sonia, it is not surprising that she has moved on, even during the course of this interview, from the position described here to the next step in her career with Johnson & Johnson. In the summer of 2011, Sonia was promoted to Senior Supply Chain Network Planner for McNeil Consumer Healthcare which is the largest consumer company within the Johnson & Johnson family of companies, manufacturing and marketing well known drugs such as Tylenol, Sudafed, Benadryl, Rolaids, Motrin, and Zyrtec. This will call upon Sonia's experience up to this date as a quality expert, and will allow her to branch out into the management of the materials, manufacturing, and marketing flow for entire systems. Since these products rely on numerous J&J locations as well as suppliers from across the continents, Sonia will continue to be asked to make good use of her global skills set. We are happy to wish her the best in her new position, knowing that it will certainly not be her last promotion!

What can we learn from Sonia Gaitan?

1. It is striking that so many alums in this study found their way to the IEP largely because of high school outreach efforts. In Sonia's case, an IEP student came to one of her science classes in her senior year and told about the program. He was a Rhode Island Hispanic immigrant himself, majoring in chemical engineering and Spanish, telling her that she could do the same. And that is exactly what she did. Would that have happened without the high school presentation? Maybe. Maybe not.

2. It is also striking that so many IEP students remain in close contact with each other after graduation. Sonia tells us that they are like a club or a family and that the IEP bond is a significant and permanent part of their lives. Having the friendship privilege with Sonia through Facebook, I can readily see that she has many friends and that the ties reflected in her photos represent two major groups. Number one is her family with whom she is extremely close. Number two is the IEP. As pointed out in several of the other case studies in this volume, a bond is formed through the common rigorous curriculum, communal living in the IEP House, and the shared experiences of studying, living and working abroad. IEP students are bilingual, cross-culturally proficient, flexible, worldly, mobile, risk-taking, ambitious and they are rightfully proud of it.

3. We can also learn from Sonia how important and productive it is to extend a hand to students from

disadvantaged backgrounds. As mentioned above, Sonia was able to enter URI through its special Talent Development Program, which provided help in securing a Pell Grant, enabled her to take jump-start courses prior to the fall semester of her freshman year, and offered extensive tutoring and mentoring. She also participated in a week-long NSF funded seminar during that first summer designed to support, mentor, and encourage young women in engineering. This program introduced her to women faculty and upper class students in the College of Engineering, all of whom would also serve in a mentoring capacity.

4. Sonia speaks of the "soft skills" that are acquired through the IEP and yet tend to be lacking in students remaining with the standard undergraduate engineering education. This is suggested by other IEP alums as well and is commonly accepted by our leadership and yet inadequately enumerated, defined or promoted. When abroad for a full year, IEP students must learn to deal with day-to-day issues on their own; they must be prepared to enter a new workplace in a strange country and non-English-speaking environment, where practice is often shaped by different cultural values. They must learn to thrive in an environment where each day presents a set of challenges, and each day means learning how to be a good American, a good colleague, an effective worker, all outside of one's traditional comfort zone. The result is a spirit of independence, a growing self-confidence, and a respect and tolerance for difference, all of which are keys to working globally.

For Sonia, a Global Engineer: *has multiple languages, past experience living, studying and working in other cultures and international business experience along with technical expertise. Global engineers are sooner able to see the Big Picture across multiple departments and countries.*

Christina and Michael Smith

Chris and Mike Smith with their two daughters,
at their home in Jamestown, Rhode Island

Studying abroad and internships are necessary to give students the opportunity to live life from a different perspective and bring that knowledge with them into the workforce. The IEP is a great model and I feel my personal and professional success is a result of that experience. I've actually often wondered if I would even be an engineer had it not been for the IEP. – **Christina Smith**

My year abroad had a profound effect on many aspects of my life. It increased my independence, strengthened friendships, and exposed me to many diverse cultures and situations. – **Michael Smith**

79

Name: Christina Petersen Smith
Born: 1978
High School: North Kingstown, Rhode Island
IEP Degrees: BA in German; BS in Mechanical Engineering, 2001
Current position: Manager of Strategic Projects, Viega, LLC, Wichita, Kansas, Attendorn, Germany
Past Position: Product Marketing Manager, Texas Instruments Corp., Attleboro, Massachusetts

Name: Michael Smith
Born: 1978
High School: Highland, New York
IEP Degrees: BA in German; BS in Electrical Engineering, 2001
Graduate Degree: University of Massachusetts, MS in Computer Engineering
Current position: Principal Electrical Engineer, BAE Systems, Inc.

In this chapter we will look at the unusual lives and careers of Christina Petersen Smith and Michael Smith who now live and work out of their home in the town of Jamestown, Rhode Island, on Conanicut Island, where they are also raising their two daughters. One would hardly imagine a scenic island in Narragansett Bay as a place for global business or defense and aerospace research and development. But Mike and Chris are engaged in precisely that, she as Manager of Strategic Projects for Viega, LLC, a German manufacturer of components for heating and water distribution systems, and he as Principal Electrical Engineer for BAE Systems, Incorporated. It is intriguing to see how Chris and Mike, who both graduated from the IEP in 2001, have been able to create such a balance to their lives in this time of constant change and intense competition. Of course, we will also ask what role the IEP and their international experiences played in the process. How did they get where they are? What role does their preparation as global

80

engineers play for them in their work, at their island home, with their two small children, in the scenic town of Jamestown, Rhode Island?

Christina grew up in Jamestown, Michael in Highland, New York. They were both excellent high school students, competitive athletes, the children of families with solid values who expected their offspring to acquire a university education. Because both excelled as math and science students, the idea of engineering was strongly encouraged, a course of study which was natural for Mike, but less so for Chris who understood that engineering was still very much male-dominated. As solid all-round students with multiple interests, both were a little reluctant about the one-sidedness of the engineering curriculum and the fear of eventually being stuck alone with a computer in a cubicle. Transcending these issues would be among the strongest reasons for both Mike and Chris to opt for the IEP. Its curriculum would take an extra year, but it would allow them to study a language and culture with engineering and spend a full year abroad, and, as Mike says, develop the other side of the brain. For both, the IEP would be valuable in and of itself, but it would also open doors to more career options and change their lives.

It is important to note that the IEP was the differentiator for both Mike and Chris when it came time to choose their college or university. It helped that both were offered merit-based scholarships, but they would have had that support elsewhere too. When looking at schools, therefore, they were in the market for something more than a straight engineering education, especially Chris. She well remembers, as do I, that she and her dad came to URI for one of its information sessions, despite a very heavy snowfall. There she had the chance to speak with me and the assistant dean of engineering, Richard Vandeputte. We, of course, shared our enthusiasm for the IEP, explaining that she could do a language degree with her engineering degree and complete an internship abroad, and also that one-third of the IEP students were women. On that day she dropped her preconceived notions of engineering as a narrow and boring

81

course of study. Once she had determined that a program like the IEP would not be possible at the several other schools where she had been accepted, she committed to attending URI in the fall, the university which originally had been her "back-up school."

Chris and Mike both took full advantage of the IEP and its infrastructure during their URI years. They were both excellent students, whether in German class, advanced mechanics, or digital electronics. Both also sought out other IEP sponsored opportunities such as summer internships. Mike spent one summer working for a biomedical technology division of Germany's Bayer AG in Tarrytown, New York, and completed a six-month internship with the TRW Corporation in Radolfzell, Germany. Chris went to Tulsa, Oklahoma for a summer internship with the Hilti Corporation, for whom she would also intern in Liechtenstein during her year abroad. When the IEP offered a two-week study tour in Germany enabling students to visit our partner university in Braunschweig and several of our affiliated companies, they both signed on. As a matter of fact, it was the study tour in Germany that enabled them to meet, develop a friendship and the basis for their marriage shortly after graduation. (Chris and Mike, by the way, represent just one of several "IEP marriages.") Mike and Chris also attended URI's German Summer School of the Atlantic, enabling them to make greater progress with their German language before going abroad for one year.

Mike and Chris also played a key role in helping me to decide to go forward with the plans for the IEP House, an on-campus residential and administrative facility for students and faculty in the program. I was frankly facing a dilemma at the time, not knowing whether it would be wise to invest time and donor monies in a rundown fraternity house which had been vacated. The concept of an IEP living/learning community was appealing, but the building needed an enormous amount of work and the project could only succeed if we could be sure that students would opt to live there. Mike and Chris encouraged me and Mike conducted an extensive survey of our IEP students, proving

82

to me that the demand was there. I am not sure if I would have had the courage to take on this challenge without their encouragement and willingness to help. Mike also developed a 3D computer model of the IEP house, while the actual house was still under renovation, and presented a virtual tour of the house during the inaugural IEP Colloquium. At that time, he also launched the first version of the IEP Web site. They were not only among the early planners, but also charter residents and charter members of the IEP student House Council, which would set the residential policies for this very successful arm of the program. Today the IEP living/learning community comprises a two building complex at the entrance to campus, where the program is managed, where 76 students live and which also includes a full dining program. The IEP housing program has become a model for higher education residential living and has served to inspire similar special housing opportunities on the URI campus.

I do not wish to portray Chris and Mike as "IEP nerds" by any means, for they were also both active in other university activities and causes. Mike was a Teaching Assistant for the Physics Department and was active in electrical engineering organizations such as IEEE. Mike also played on both the URI and TU-Braunschweig Ultimate Frisbee teams, which became an important social and cultural experience during his time in Braunschweig. Chris was an admissions office worker for her four years on campus, which included service as a campus tour guide for prospective students and their families. She was also active in intramural sports and President of the URI chapter of the Society of Women Engineers.

Upon graduation, Mike and Chris both found good jobs, Mike at BAE Systems in Nashua, New Hampshire, where he is still employed today, and Chris at the Texas Instruments Corporation in Attleboro, Massachusetts. Once married, they made their first home midway between their two places of employment for commuting convenience. Logistics became more complicated, however, when Chris had a chance to join a German company in Massachusetts where she could put her language and culture skills to good use. She loved her new position, but was asked after two years to relocate to Kansas where Viega had just taken over another company. Though moving seemed beyond the realm of possibility due to Mike's position in New Hampshire, he was able to convince his bosses that he could do his work remotely just as effectively as being in the office in New Hampshire. They thus moved to Wichita, Kansas where they would spend the next three years, Chris at Viega as a product manager and Mike as a principal engineer for a Virginia branch of BAE Systems working from their home in Wichita.

As is often the case with engineers in general and IEP grads in specific, Mike and Chris found themselves migrating somewhat from their original career directions. For Chris it would mean becoming more of a global business leader and less of an engineer. For Mike it would mean not going to work for a company requiring his German experience, but rather moving toward work with increasingly sophisticated technologies in the national defense and aerospace industry. Chris and Mike are nevertheless both insistent that their IEP education has been extremely valuable and continues to be put to good use.

Mike makes it very clear that his in-depth exposure to another culture through another language prepared him to deal with the multi-cultural and diverse nature of his professional workplace. He also credits his IEP education for much of his independence and problem solving skills, the ability to tolerate and deal with difference and change, and the ability to bring people together and create effective teams. Though Mike works at home, he is an integral part of several teams whose members might be in New Hampshire, Virginia, Washington D.C. or any number of other locations around the country. His teams meet regularly by means of teleconference and, as he points out, the cultural make-up of the groups is diverse in a variety of ways. To meet their targets, electrical engineers like Mike have to coordinate with engineers from other disciplines, with management, with business leaders, those responsible for manufacturing, and, of course, also with the customers. Mike has gained a reputation in his company as a good team builder, a person who can appreciate the contribution of others and who can recognize and transcend cultural, regional, and disciplinary barriers in order to get the job done more efficiently and smoothly. He feels that his skills in these areas are superior to those of most American engineers, and he believes that it is his in-depth international education that has made a very real difference.

Chris works for the U.S. subsidiary of a German company and finds direct application for her German IEP education, both technically and cross-culturally. Viega is known for its innovative connection technologies for the heating and plumbing business, with particular applications for radiant heating and water distribution systems. Viega employs 3000 people worldwide, with approximately 500 employees in the United States and North American headquarters in Wichita, Kansas. Chris began her career with Viega as a product manager, responsible for all aspects of the product life cycle including determining customer requirements, technical attributes, market introduction strategies, product maintenance and phase out. In this capacity she had to manage cross-functional and cross-cultural teams to improve time to market with successful products.

Her job was made especially challenging as a result of Viega's purchase of an existing manufacturing facility in Wichita in 2005. The German acquisition of this plant was very stressful over the first few years, with much of the tension attributable to cultural difference. Viega is a family owned enterprise which had retained all of its research and development and manufacturing in Germany up to this point and had no prior experience with manufacturing abroad. It is not surprising, therefore, that a company from Germany with its own well-established practices would encounter obstacles when imposing its own culture on an existing manufacturing facility with its equally well-established way of doing things.

Thanks to her IEP education, including her year abroad and her internships with Hilti, Chris understood the issues and was and is able to play a key mediator role. She is one of a small number of Americans in the company who speaks German and who understands how, for example, the German up-front and blunt style of communication can be a problem for Kansans or how the Kansas eagerness to please can be misinterpreted by Germans. With the help of employees like Chris, a strong executive management team and a CEO with considerable experience working globally, the company was able to make its transition and successfully integrate the parent company's best supply chain practices while also becoming a strong part of the overall global R&D team responsible for the products manufactured in North America.

Chris currently is Manager of Strategic Projects for Viega, a job which she is able to do mainly out of her home in Rhode Island. In this position she is a student of trends in an industry which is impacted by continually changing standards and regulations. It is her job to identify new business opportunities, to network and make contacts with potentially new North American business partners. It is also her job to be sure that the engineering and management teams in both Kansas and Germany fully understand these opportunities. This means a fair amount of travel, constant contact with her team and with the company management, but not so much that she and Mike are not able to spend the time needed to raise their two daughters at home. Chris believes that the current configuration of her job is somewhat of a compromise. Were she to have stayed in Wichita she might have advanced more professionally, but that would have meant a sacrifice for her family. Right now that is a fully acceptable compromise which will certainly keep the doors open for other career opportunities, should she seek such when her daughters are a bit older.

What can we learn from the Smiths?

1. As with the other IEP alums in this study, Mike and Chris Smith believe strongly that the IEP education provided them with benefits of a life-long nature. The added dimensions include a broader engineering education, an appreciation for how their disciplines are practiced in different cultural environments, but also a set of skills that apply to life in many ways. Mike and Chris learned the value of risk taking through the IEP, and they also learned to navigate outside of their comfort zones and to take on problems and challenges when the network of support is not readily available. They learned independence and creativity, which are so apparent in their lives today. They also learned tolerance and appreciation for otherness, and these have become assets for success in their careers on an almost daily basis.

2. From Chris and Mike, the IEP learns once again the importance of outreach to gifted students at the high school level. Neither really knew about the IEP before coming to campus, but both were in search of a differentiator that would assure them of an education beyond engineering in and of itself. Both had been accepted by several other schools, some of which were by reputation far more prestigious than URI, and both chose URI specifically because of the IEP. One might wish that today's high school student would know about programs such as the IEP well in advance of decision time, but this is still not the case. School outreach is as important today as it was ten years ago, if we hope to attract more gifted students to programs like the IEP.

3. We can also learn something from Chris and Mike about the bond that is created among young people who have an extensive study and work experience abroad in common. It would, of course, be foolish to suggest that the Smiths became a couple solely because of the IEP. However, a totally integrated foreign study program with acquisition of a new

language, in-depth encounter with another culture, and joint confrontation of any number of challenges and discoveries provides a set of common experiences, values, and skills which contribute greatly to the core needed for a life-long partnership. Both Mike and Chris believe that the IEP was definitely a life-changing experience. The fact that they went through this together is a part of their make-up as individuals and as a couple.

Though only a small number marry each other, IEP students and graduates all enjoy a commonality and bond that begins with their undergraduate years and lasts far into the future. IEP grads tend to stay in touch with the program and with each other, not the least sign of which is the amount commonly shared by IEPers through Facebook and LinkedIn.

4. Though Mike and Chris both come from family backgrounds which value and teach tolerance, respect, and teamwork, they both believe that each of these was strengthened as a result of their IEP education. Mike points out that his colleagues from Virginia do not necessarily share the same cultural perspectives as colleagues from New Hampshire, and that BAE Systems needs to understand how these differences can stand in the way of its goals. He also appreciates the fact that a team member may have an excellent idea, but might not be able to communicate that idea, whether due to communication style or a language barrier. Chris too understands that each culture tends to have a distinct communication style which can, at times, be severely misunderstood. As a result of fine-tuning their cross-cultural skills by in-depth study in another language and culture, both Chris and Mike have become known in their workplaces as good mediators, good team builders, and good problem solvers.

5. From Chris and Mike, as with the others in this volume, we learn again the importance of application for the language learning process. Had German not been tied to engineering, internships, and study abroad, neither Mike nor Chris would have been likely language learners at URI. Because it was tied to a tangible larger goal, however, they not only studied German, but attended the summer immersion program, participated in a German study tour, spent a full-year abroad and completed full majors in the language.

6. We learn also from Mike and Chris that graduates might or might not find direct application in their careers for their recently acquired language skills. We should be pleased when that is the case, as it is for Chris, but we should not be distraught if not. Bilingualism, while valuable from many points of view, is just one outcome of the program. Mike, for example, only occasionally uses German, when a relevant scientific article crosses his desk, or when colleagues consult him to translate something of value to their work. But, as seen above, it is the process of becoming bilingual and the experience of being bilingual that have opened doors to lasting cross-cultural experience and left a lasting impression.

For Chris: *A global engineer is someone who is aware of cultural differences, understands the impact these have on interactions and is able to overcome these challenges to successfully develop products and processes.*

For Mike: *A global engineer is one whose technical skills are decoupled from their physical location. They can work anywhere. Common characteristics of a global engineer likely include cultural awareness and openness to an atypical career path.*

Addendum: Shortly before going to press with this volume, Mike Smith decided, after 10 years with BAE

Systems, that it would be wise to make a professional move. His new position is with a Rhode Island based company, Applied Radar, in North Kingstown, RI. He sees it as an opportunity to apply his skills in a very different kind of environment and contribute to the development and growth of a currently small firm. As mentioned in the introduction, the stories in this volume are incomplete and represent only the early stages of this collection of exciting careers.

Daniel Fischer

The IEP opened up the doors to the global marketplace, and showed me that there are tremendous opportunities outside of the U.S. as well. The experiences gave me the opportunity to work for a world-renowned company (Siemens) designing ultra high-tech medical devices (MRI) that have a meaningful impact on the lives of millions of people.

Born: North Kingstown, Rhode Island
High School: North Kingstown, Rhode Island
IEP: BA in German; BS in Electrical Engineering, 2002
Graduate Degree: Universität Bayreuth, MBA in Healthcare Management, 2010
Current position: Product Manager, MRI Systems, Siemens AG, Erlangen, Germany
Past Position: Engineer, Research & Development, MRI Systems, Siemens AG. Erlangen, Germany
Personal: Married to Maria Jung

After a recent attack of extreme dizziness, I found myself on my back being inserted into an ominous looking piece of technology in our local hospital in Rhode Island, all to ensure that I had suffered from Vertigo and not something far more serious. While being prepared for this intimidating experience, I caught sight of the word Siemens and, as IEP Director Emeritus, could take comfort in the fact that this miraculous MRI (Magnetic Resonance Imaging) machine was a product of a well-known division of a German company with whom we had been placing interns for some years, and where one of our graduates, Daniel Fischer, is a Product Manager. Ironically I had just been in contact with Dan as a candidate for this study, and he had explained his work to me as developer and manager of MRI instruments in some detail. Though I have no expertise in this area, I nevertheless gained confidence knowing that our hospital had chosen an MRI device from the world leader in that technology, and that I indirectly had some kind of personal relationship with this machine and Siemens Medical Solutions. I knew Daniel and I knew that this was over a billion dollar business for Siemens, with approximately 1200 people working on this technology. I was glad that the MRI gave me a good report, and I am very glad and proud to be able to tell about Daniel Fischer in this chapter.

Dan is one of a handful of managers in the Magnetic Resonance Imaging product definition group in Erlangen, Germany, which determines the next steps for MRI development, based on the advances of medical knowledge and technology, but also on the market and needs of the market. As a manager, he is currently the "product owner" for three systems, and he must ensure that these specific devices make good business sense and succeed in the marketplace. The product manager must work closely with the technology development side to define new accessories, applications, features, or entire new systems, and he must collaborate closely with the marketing teams and serve as their technical expert. In short, he has a huge responsibility for a young engineer not even ten years in the workplace.

Dan Fischer was born and raised in North Kingstown, Rhode Island, just a few miles from the University of Rhode Island. He attributes his strong work ethic and his path to the IEP and subsequent successes to his parents, but also to his high school German classes, the athletics program, and his early interest in computers. Taking four years of German in high school, which included lots of exposure to things German, gave him a head start for the German IEP. His active participation in athletics, in cross-country running, basketball, and baseball, provided him with good teamwork and leadership skills and also a love of competition. He was also exposed to computers at an early age when he learned *that a computer is nothing to be scared of; it does exactly what you tell it to do (this helps when admitting mistakes/fixing errors), and many decisions can be easy to make, if the path leading to them is well thought out.*

Dan never faced the problem encountered by others when choosing an academic path or a college. He knew from high school speakers and from his older brother, who was already in the IEP program, that the University of Rhode Island offered a curriculum through which he could pursue both his interest in German and computers. He knew that it was "a tough program," but he had already learned not to shy from challenges, and he believed that he could pursue both interests in this way, with hopes that it would help him find his way personally and professionally. *After finishing high school and not necessarily knowing exactly what I wanted to study, I realized that I had an asset that could not be ignored: a solid foundation in a foreign language (German) and a genuine interest in continuing to learn the language. The IEP offered a chance to expand on these language skills and combine them with a degree in technology, another major interest of mine.* Dan was accepted by both URI and Northeastern, but the IEP was what he wanted, so the decision to attend URI was easy.

Dan maintained his rigorous work ethic as an undergraduate, majoring in German and Electrical Engineering. He remained active athletically through intramural

93

basketball, and worked both summers and part-time during the academic year to help pay for his college expenses. By the summer of 2000, he had enough computer background to be able to intern as a programmer with a Rhode Island company which makes, among other things, specialized printers for the medical industry (Astro-Med, Inc.) He also worked as a computer lab assistant during his last two years at URI.

Dan spent his fourth URI year (2000-2001) in Germany, studying for the fall semester in Braunschweig and then interning for Siemens Medical Solutions in Forchheim. He describes this year as *the most valuable learning experience that I got out of my college years.* He learned very rapidly upon his arrival in Braunschweig that he could communicate in German, but that he had a long ways to go if he really wanted to be proficient on a professional level. His determination to reach this plane meant learning to get out of his comfort zone each day, not to spend his free time with fellow Americans, but to get to know the German students and immerse himself in the culture and language. Following these guidelines, which included joining German intramural sports teams, Dan made tremendous progress with his German and was ready for his internship with Siemens by the second half of his year abroad.

His internship was with the Computer Tomography (CT) group of Siemens Medical Solutions based in Forchheim, Germany, where he worked from March to August 2001 in the hardware integration team and developed a few tools to aide in the integration and testing process for a new product. Aside from learning a little bit about programming, he was able to get a first-hand look at what is required to get an incredibly complex product ready for clinical testing, and how the process for a development project is performed.

Dan benefitted greatly from this second stage of the year abroad, where he was required to be on his own, responsible for his own housing, meals, and other aspects of daily life, and where he was the sole American intern. Dan greatly appreciates having been pushed out of his "comfort zone" and required to make it on his own merits. During this time he made great strides linguistically and also developed his "cross-cultural antennae" and grew to understand that American students and Americans in general live in a very "protected aquarium" with far too little appreciation for the interests and perspectives of people in other parts of the world. At the same time, Dan created a good impression of himself with his Siemens supervisors, which would mean the doors were opening for career opportunities once he graduated.

Dan returned to URI for his final year of the program. Though, as he tell us, he would never have given it consideration before going to Germany, he found himself that year wondering if he might be able to get back to Siemens for more experience. Pursuing it on his own, Dan secured a second internship with Siemens for the summer of 2002, just prior to his final semester at URI. This time, he interned with the MRI group in a product development team and developed software to aid in the test of new hardware components for the MRI control system. As he tells us, this job was much more "hands-on" and involved contact with the technology and electronics that goes into developing new hardware components. This internship also had a significant people component to it - he learned that in complex projects in which there are many (100+) developers involved, effective communication is an absolute prerequisite to making sure that things move smoothly.

Dan obviously performed well during both stints at Siemens. After the second internship was finished and Dan was back at URI for his final semester, the team leader from the MRI group contacted him saying that a position in his group would be available, and invited him to apply. Soon he had a telephone interview with the team leader and the department head, and then not too long after that, he was flown over to Erlangen for a round of interviews with human resources, the head of development, and finally the head of the business unit. A week later he was offered the job, which he started in February 2003.

Dan works in a very international laboratory, but German nevertheless remains the almost sole language of communication with his team members. He would not have been considered for his position with Siemens in Germany, were he not a fluent speaker. As he relates to us, he would not have the respect of his colleagues if he were not able to meet them on their linguistic turf. *My main language at work with my colleagues is German. This is a major asset because as a speaker of the language, you can much better understand the culture and also how people in that language generally think. This offers a tremendous amount of credibility and trust among my colleagues.*

It goes without saying as well, that Dan would not be where he is today without having gained an appreciation for cultural difference and for strategies bridging the differences in modes of thought and operation between Germans and Americans. It goes without saying that Dan is both bilingual and bicultural. When asked about his ability and role as a cross-cultural communicator, it is ironic that Dan answered from the German perspective, with reference to differences between colleagues in China and Erlangen. In short, cross-cultural mediation between Germans and Americans is such second nature to him now, that he no longer considers it a separate task and did not mention it in his answer.

Dan sees cultural understanding as paramount. He learned very early that saying something, whether in English or German, does not ensure that the listener grasps the meaning as the speaker intends it, and that this is very often conditioned by culture. He also learned through his appreciation of such differences to be a better listener as well as a more thoughtful speaker, and that there is often more than one way to approach and solve a problem. *Different people have different ways of doing things, and in understanding their motivation behind this, you can see if there are then aspects that you can apply to your solution. The "foreign" engineers also have the benefit in learning from you. In that sense, you also learn how to communicate your ideas to different audiences.*

Dan feels indebted to the IEP. He is confident that he would have performed well as an engineer, with or without the IEP. But he attributes much of his current status to benefits accrued from the program. The IEP provided Dan with his language skills and the basis for his cross-cultural expertise. And it opened many doors for him. He reminds us repeatedly that he would not be part of Siemens and its ultra high-tech medical devices without his IEP education. And like other IEP grads, the program has affected his personal life as well. While growing more and more at home in Erlangen, Dan has also met and fallen in love with his life's partner, Maria Jung, with whom he will be married in the fall of 2011. Looking back to his high school days in North Kingstown, his love of baseball, German classes, and his Texas Instruments computer, Dan tells us that the IEP enabled him to put it all together for a very exciting and meaningful career and life's path.

What can we learn from Daniel Fischer?
1. Dan Fischer's case once again drives home the value and relevance of the URI motto: Think Big We Do. From the perspective of a seventeen year old in a high school classroom in North Kingstown, Rhode Island, holding a leadership research and development position in Germany with a company like Siemens AG, and helping to develop the latest in medical diagnostic systems may seem like an unimaginable leap. Yet, Dan acquired the skills during his URI IEP education to do exactly that. His degree in electrical engineering, his fluency in German and his network of contacts developed during his internship opened several doors, enabling him to compete with the best and prove himself as an engineer with global leadership capabilities.
2. As an alum who has achieved success in a very competitive realm of ultra high-technology for one of the world's largest companies, Dan has a right to pass on wisdom to us and our students. His words provide encouragement that programs like the IEP are very appropriate, but he also reminds us to continually educate our colleagues and our students regarding the absolute necessity of a global

education. *It should be made clear to engineering students that they will be creating, designing, or manufacturing products that will be most likely sold and competing with similar products of equal or greater quality from around the world.* One might argue that these words give expression to the obvious. But American students still live in a very sheltered and culturally limited environment, generally without the knowledge that they will be working in and for a global market and expected to compete with the best from the entire world.

3. Dan Fischer, like most others in this study, helps us to appreciate the extent to which an IEP education breeds personal self-confidence and the ability to not only think big, but take the risks necessary for success. Dan wanted to study both German and engineering, but was not sure that he could do both. The IEP and its infrastructure provided the path and gave him the encouragement and support to follow such a curriculum. He always knew that he wanted to put his computer skills to use in a way that would make a difference for society. By the time of graduation, he could not only see the potential for making that dream a reality, but could also dare to seek professional opportunities with one of the world's leading companies at its headquarters outside of the United States.

4. Dan Fischer joins the others in this study who demonstrate that a curriculum such as the IEP serves as a magnet for students with multiple talents and interests. He took four years of German in high school and wanted desperately to continue his language and culture study. But he was also a math and science whiz with a passion for computers. Had he not found the IEP, it is likely that he would have majored solely in a purely technical field. That would have meant no German courses, no study or internship abroad, and no career with Siemens.

Dan Fischer defines the global engineer as: *someone who can not only build working relationships with foreign colleagues but also earn their trust, and who understands that there can be more than one way to solve a problem, regardless of what it is. A global engineer needs to be open-minded and flexible.*

Sharon Ruggieri

At the IEP I started to gain confidence in myself and as a consequence I began to succeed. I found a great group of people who supported me through the IEP program and I started to learn from my friends from other countries. I learned to embrace cultural differences and how to adapt my behavior to effectively communicate/work with different cultures.

As a result of the opportunities at the IEP I began to believe I could reach even higher and this led me to the Fulbright program and later to MIT. Before the IEP my universe was limited to my state; now my education and professional career has no borders.

Age: 26
High School: Cranston, Rhode Island
IEP Degrees: BA in Spanish; BS in Mechanical Engineering, 2007
Graduate Degrees: MBA, MIT Sloan School of Management, 2011
Current position: Search in progress
Past Position: Fulbright Scholar and entrepreneurial consultant, Mexico

Like each of the IEP alums presented in this volume, Sharon Ruggieri's case is unique and impressive, but, unlike the others, she is a more recent grad (2007) and has yet to hold a regular position. This does not mean that she has not been busy and without challenges, achievements, and rewards. Nor does it mean that she has not had enticing job opportunities. Quite to the contrary, Sharon could have gone to work upon graduation for the aerospace industry, but held off, hoping that her pending application for a post-graduate Fulbright program would enable her to go back to Mexico. Sharon had decided that more education abroad with a focus on business study and business experience would enhance her profile and provide greater opportunities in the long run than taking an immediate engineering position. And fortunately her courageous decision paid off. She did win the Fulbright award, she did spend a year in Mexico, and she was right that this would lead to other good things. Her unusual background, including impressive work and study in Spain and Mexico, total fluency in Spanish, and a year of Fulbright support made her a successful candidate for admission to one of the world's top three graduate programs in business. In May 2011 she earned the MBA from MIT's Sloan School of Management.

Sharon Ruggieri is a Rhode Islander, raised and educated in the city of Cranston. She tells us that three things were especially influential in her early life, shaping her as a good candidate for the IEP. From her active participation in Girl Scouts she gained confidence in herself as a young woman and learned to work hard, practice kindness toward others, and not to be afraid to think and dream big. From her enthusiastic and very dedicated high school physics teacher she learned to love science, to strive to achieve academically, and to open her mind to the idea of engineering. She is also indebted to her parents who encouraged her throughout her life. Her dad is a URI-educated engineer, as are three of her uncles, so studying engineering at URI was not a big surprise. Her parents (her mother is also a URI grad) did not study abroad or have a fascination for languages like Sharon, but they helped pique her interest by taking in exchange students from whom she learned to love Spanish, to value cultural difference and to want to go abroad herself.

When faced with college choices, Sharon assumed at first that she would not be able to reconcile her love of language and culture with engineering. She knew that she could do well in either area, but had believed that college meant choosing one over the other. But Sharon was fortunate to hear a presentation at her school about the IEP which surprised her with the opportunity to major in both engineering and language. The fact that this would take an extra year did not bother her in the least. She knew immediately that this program was for her! As she tells us: *I was equally passionate about my Spanish and Physics classes in high school and could not decide which I would pursue in college. Someone from the IEP gave a presentation at my high school and I was excited to learn I could do both so I applied to the IEP.*

With the IEP as the differentiating and deciding factor, Sharon applied solely to URI and entered as a freshman in 2002. Very much like the others described in this volume, she took full advantage of the program and its infrastructure. She lived in the supportive atmosphere of the IEP House with other students pursuing engineering and language and with exchange students who would give her the chance to practice her Spanish with native speakers. Determined to be bilingual by the end of her studies at URI, she was not afraid to make mistakes or to be "lost" when spending time with her classmates from Spain. *Each year I was more immersed in Spanish and by the 5th year (which I spent physically at URI) about 85% of what I spoke during each day was in Spanish. The IEP environment made this immersion possible by giving me access to native speakers, a diversity of language classes, conversation clubs and promoting foreign language activities (meals, movie nights, trips, etc).*

Sharon also took full advantage of internship opportunities for professional, personal, and cross-cultural growth. She won a fellowship to spend the summer of 2005 at the Universidad de Puerto Rico, Mayagüez Campus (UPRM) through the URI Transportation Program. There she worked with a professor on a research project investigating the behavior of fiber reinforced polymer (FRP) tubes as a tool to prevent corrosion of concrete columns, used most commonly for bridge columns submerged in corrosive salt water. This was her first experience in a native speaking Spanish environment, as well as her first engineering experience outside a URI laboratory. This prepared her both practically and mentally for her IEP semester that fall at the IEP's partner university in Spain, the Universidad de Navarra, School of Engineering, TECNUN, in San Sebastian, where she took engineering classes entirely in Spanish and was the only exchange student from an English speaking country. Following the semester in Spain, Sharon completed a six-month internship as a Quality Engineering Intern at a division of Texas Instruments in Aguascalientes, Mexico, where she was responsible for analyzing rejected parts from an automotive production line and coming up with process improvements to reduce the failure rate. Although her experience in Spain was positive overall, Sharon was immediately taken with the style of life in Latin America. She felt immediately accepted and welcome and embraced the warmth, openness, and vibrant spirit of the Mexican people, qualities which are not always readily apparent among New Englanders!

Sharon made tremendous progress toward her goals while living and working abroad. She enjoyed her experiences greatly, even though it was not easy. As she tells us: *Living abroad led to so many challenges! At first I missed my U.S. products, food, TV shows, stores, etc. Sometimes I was frustrated by the differences in culture that I did not understand and my head hurt from so much Spanish. I struggled to be included in social groups abroad, I got lost a lot trying to find simple things like a bus stop or an ATM, and I missed deadlines because I heard a different date then what the professor said. I could go on and on but the positive side is that the only way to overcome these challenges is through practice; you just need to make lots of*

103

mistakes before you start to figure out how to get by and eventually thrive.

Despite, or perhaps because of the challenges, Sharon did thrive in the experiences abroad, immersing herself in the language and concomitantly in the deeper cultural nuances, establishing friendships and building a network of contacts along the way. Today Sharon speaks Spanish with the accuracy and pronunciation of a native, and she feels readily at home in all Spanish-speaking environments, especially in Latin America, where she finds people to be open, vibrant, warm, and very expressive. *Before the IEP I only spoke in English and when I left I lived my life primarily in Spanish. This was a major change for me! Most of my environment is in Spanish now including my music, movies, and conversations with friends. I am also now more willing to try new things (including different foods), and I tend to not judge people so quickly because now I understand the sources of our differences and am generally more able to recognize assets and opportunities among peoples' differences.*

It is not surprising that the IEP has opened doors for Sharon, given her passion for engineering and Spanish and her drive to succeed. As mentioned above, Sharon applied for the Fulbright Binational Business Program in her last year at URI, with hopes of returning to Mexico for a second full year. She had a good offer from the aerospace industry in Connecticut, but decided against it, even though the fellowship had not yet materialized. Sharon was betting that her past experience and unusual IEP degree credentials would make her very competitive for the Fulbright and fortunately she was right.

Sharon spent the year after graduation (September 2007 – June 2008) in Mexico, taking MBA evening courses in finance, economics, leadership, and statistics at EGADE Business School (Escuela de Graduados en Administracion y Direccion de Empresas) in Monterrey, Mexico, which she found to be an excellent complement to her background in engineering. At the same time she interned with Banorte Financial Group as a Fulbright-Garcia Robles Grantee in

104

structured finance. At Banorte she received proposals for real estate investment projects from international development firms, including shopping malls, office buildings and government infrastructure. Her task was to analyze the proposals and write reports analyzing the feasibility and value of the projects for the bank's directors.

Feeling very much at home in Mexico, Sharon decided not to return to Rhode Island immediately after the Fulbright year, but to stay on for a period with a company she had come to know during her prior internship in Aguascalientes. There she served as a business development consultant for an entrepreneur she had met while working for Texas Instruments. She did this to gain experience in growing a business beyond its initial levels of success. Her task was to assist in developing a plan to market the business, standardize processes, develop suppliers and create a strategy for long-term growth.

Once again, Sharon could have gone to work as an engineer, this time with a very nice offer in Mexico from a Japanese car manufacturer. But, with her appetite whetted for more background and expertise in global business, she decided once again to postpone her career in the workplace and to think and dream bigger. Knowing that her long-term goals could better be met with an MBA degree from one of the more prestigious business schools in the U.S., she applied for the MBA program at MIT's Sloan School of Management, where she was indeed accepted and where she completed her degree in May 2011. Sloan generally accepts candidates with prior work experience of at least five years, but an exception was made in her case thanks to her unusual background, which included two undergraduate degrees, engineering expertise, fluency in Spanish, prior coursework in business, and extensive professional experience abroad. In short, the IEP and her drive, passion, and willingness to take calculated risks made her a very attractive candidate.

To her pleasure, Sharon's Sloan class enabled her to continue her pursuit of excellence in conjunction with Latin America. Many of her classmates (approximately 40 of her class of 300) were from that part of the world and she became very active with the larger Latin American community at MIT. Even in Cambridge, Massachusetts she could use her Spanish on a daily basis. Also, she was able to bring her experience to bear for the benefit of others. She served, for example, as the Vice-president of the MIT Sloan Latin Business Club, which promotes MIT in Latin America and educates MIT students on the growth of the business sector in Latin America. She was also the President of the MIT Latin American Conference, an annual symposium attracting business leaders from all over Latin America to speak at MIT. (See www.mitlac.com for information about the impressive 2011 annual meeting, co-organized by Sharon and attended by approximately 400 persons.) Sharon was also able to return to Mexico for the summer of 2010 as a Sloan intern for Endeavor Global, a non-profit organization supporting high-impact entrepreneurs in developing countries. She was selected to assist a Monterrey entrepreneur develop strategies to expand his cellular telephone tower business to the U.S. market.

Sharon points out that the IEP prepared her for her goals rapidly and at a very young age when compared to her peers both inside and outside the U.S. She was the youngest person among the Fulbright Binational Business Program awardees; she was one of the youngest in her Sloan MBA class, and she was the youngest intern for the Endeavor Program in Mexico during the summer of 2010. When preparing to enter the workplace upon graduation in May 2011, recruiters from global companies were generally shocked at the extensive nature of her global experience for someone so young. Sharon is extremely grateful for the head start given to her by the IEP which opened doors for her and set off what she describes as a very positive chain reaction, beginning at URI, taking her to internship and study experiences in Puerto Rico, Spain, Mexico and then to Fulbright and MIT. *Now, as I am thinking about my next career move there is no country or industry that is off-limits. I travel around the world and think nothing of it because I am comfortable in diverse situations and prepared to handle anything.* Given her middle-class Rhode Island background and the difficulty in imagining from her high school in Cranston that she could be a major player with global entrepreneurs by the age of 26, Sharon feels that her accomplishments to date are "mind boggling." She does not hesitate to say that she would not be where she is today without the IEP.

At the time of this writing, Sharon has just completed her MBA, but has not yet decided on her next move. She is networking by way of the Sloan School, the IEP, and her many friends and past colleagues in the U.S. and Mexico. She will have a variety of choices, whether with a global firm in this country or in Mexico, or possibly with an NGA such as Endeavor. I look forward to following Sharon's career over the coming years.

What can we learn from Sharon Ruggieri?

1. Once again, Sharon's case alerts us as international educators to the importance of high school outreach. As a student passionate about both Spanish and math/science related subjects, Sharon was a natural for the program. But, believing that she would have to choose the pursuit of one area over the other at the university level, it was the presentation in her high school about the IEP that set her on her current extraordinary path. Had she not learned about the IEP that day, she may well have missed her chance to pursue her two passions simultaneously with such enthusiasm and success.

2. Sharon also reminds us of the impact that a good teacher and mentor can have. She must have had good Spanish teachers in high school to trigger her love of the language. Though, as she tells us, this was also enhanced by her parents who saw the value of hosting exchange students in their home. But special credit must also go to her high school physics teacher, whose love of teaching and passion for his/her subject area had such an enormous affect on Sharon and her choices for the future. Sharon also feels indebted to the overall URI/IEP experience

where she received an engineering education with strong emphasis on team building, and where she was directly and regularly mentored by faculty and staff, and especially by IEP Assistant Director Kathleen Maher.

3. The IEP can learn from Sharon the extent to which critical soft skills are a byproduct of its in-depth global education. Sharon, like the others in this volume, is by nature and upbringing a very motivated and hard working young woman, who would no doubt succeed with or without the IEP. Yet, as she tells us, the program not only opened doors for her, but nurtured the soft skills so necessary for today's global workplace. Through the IEP, she learned persistence in the face of adversity, and she gained enormous confidence in herself, believing that she could rise to the challenge level, always dreaming and thinking big. She also learned the value of calculated risk taking which followed from her growth in self-confidence. The IEP needs to remind itself and its students on a regular basis that the program provides the necessary soft skills that combine with the so-called hard skills to create leaders. To measure the success of a program like the IEP, all of these qualities need to be enumerated and evaluated, not just the skills that we routinely monitor with grades and a GPA. Were she to have a 4.0 grade point average, but no increase in self-confidence, no ability to take calculated risks, no inspiration to think big, no persistence in the face of difficult challenges, no tolerance for diversity, we would not be writing about her today.

4. In her interview Sharon stressed the role that her study abroad experience in Spain played in terms of personal growth and self-confidence. Coming from the typical American middle-class background and higher education system, where all needs are provided, the Spanish university system was a shock to her. In San Sebastian, she took courses with no

assignments and only one final exam at the end, and which thus demanded that she take major responsibility for her own learning. She was required to find her own living arrangements in Spain, to provide for her own meals, to make her own travel arrangements and so forth. Looking back, she believes that this experience was invaluable for her own growth and is now extremely grateful that the IEP does not take the cookie cutter approach to study abroad, whereby American students are kept together and pampered, as if they were still at home. IEP students at partner institutions abroad are expected to take courses in the language, just as their engineering students would have to do in Rhode Island. IEP students are expected to take responsibility for themselves; they do not have the benefit of a resident Rhode Island advisor, and are not allowed to live in American clusters, with all needs met. In short, they must live there as the native students do.

5. In her interview for this study, Sharon stressed that *few skills are more important than cross-cultural communication. Leadership and teamwork are very important but the success of a project depends on the ability of the team to effectively communicate. In my career I would be pressed to find a team that did not include someone from another culture, in fact, most of the time I am the only American on the team. If I am not able to understand the culture of my teammates and know how I can adapt my communication strategy to work effectively with them, then the project suffers.* Sharon readily points out that such skills are a byproduct of learning a language in-depth, of studying culture in the classroom, then immersing oneself in the native environment abroad on a longer-term basis. She also stresses that this can only come through experience, with much by trial and error. To this I would add that the IEP could and should well increase its active focus on the

theories and practice of cross-cultural communication. Too often we take it as a given that these skills will emerge as one of many end goals, but, because cross-cultural communication is less tangible and less measureable than, for example, language acquisition or knowledge of things such as finite element analysis, the topic tends to be placed on the back burner.

6. Sharon also reminds us of the necessary linkage between engineering and business, and the value of integrating the study of one with the other. It is to her credit that she chose to apply to a Fulbright program for global business as a complement to her degree in mechanical engineering, and then to the MIT MBA program. Certainly every student cannot do both, and some will opt for greater depth in technology rather than studying business. However, the two are by nature interlinked and global competitiveness will require more experts who are savvy in both areas. We need to be prepared to assist students inclined to work in this direction.

Sharon provides her definition of a Global Engineer as: *someone who strives toward solutions using math and science while working in cross-cultural teams comprised of co-workers, suppliers, customers, etc. This person works effectively with people from different countries and who speak different languages.*

Good global engineers are able to understand cultural differences and how to work effectively with these differences, as opposed to simply ignoring them. They are able to adapt to diverse situations when working in a different country. A global engineer takes advantage of resources and talent from other cultures/countries and recognizes the value of these differences as assets.

A global engineer is frequently in charge of processes or products intended for the global market where the design or solution takes into consideration the market differences.

110

Matthew J. Zimmerman

Born: 1977
High School: Framingham, Massachusetts   1995
IEP Degrees: BA in German and French; BS in Ocean Engineering, 2001
Current position: Founder and Vice President for Engineering, FarSounder Inc.
Past Position: Engineer, Pyrcon LLC.
Personal: Married to Katie Zimmerman

Matt Zimmerman preparing to install
a FarSounder sonar for testing

*The IEP made me a better engineer in that it
introduced me to other points of view. Understanding people and encouraging creativity are
important for technological leadership.*

*The IEP enforced my belief that I can achieve
great things and implement big ideas. Students
need to see that reiterated many times. The IEP
gave me the chance to live in another country
during my college career. That is an experience
that makes one think differently.*

Matthew Zimmerman breaks the stereotypes that
anyone might hold regarding engineers. He is definitely a
technologist, having graduated from URI in 2001 with a
degree in Ocean Engineering, but Matt is also an artist, a
musician, a teacher, an entrepreneur, a linguist, a global
traveler, a consummate cook, a scuba diver, and a visionary
for his community. Today he is Vice President of Engineering for a leading-edge company which he himself founded
ten years ago, but, at the same time, he maintains a
commitment to his broader interests, and to the IEP, through
which he complemented his engineering degree with a
Bachelor of Arts in French and German, and at least the
equivalent of a minor in music.

Matt Zimmerman caught the travel bug and the
desire to interact with people from other cultures while on a
high school study tour to Russia. Though he had been a
science and math buff with no real appreciation for foreign
languages up to this point, his attitude shifted dramatically
through this experience, not unlike that of Eric Sargent
when going with his high school class to Paris. When soon
thereafter looking at colleges and universities, Matt knew he
wanted engineering, but he now also wanted his education
to be international. Not knowing exactly what that would
be, but realizing that language skills were the key to
accessing other cultures, he found his answer when he
learned about the chance to study languages with
engineering at URI and to spend a year studying and
interning abroad. As with the other alums described in this

112

volume, the IEP was to become the differentiator and the deciding factor for choosing URI over other schools where he could study engineering, but where there was no infrastructure for study and work abroad comparable to that of the IEP. His final decision for URI over Carnegie Mellon was also helped by the fact that he could continue playing the upright bass at the URI Music Department.

Matt came to URI as a freshman in 1995 with his mind made up to make the absolute most of the IEP. He not only wanted to complete a program enabling him to study a language along with engineering, but a curriculum that would help him develop as broadly as possible technically, culturally, and artistically. For that reason he approached us in his second year at URI asking if he could do French as well as German and arrange international experiences in both France and Germany rather than spend the year solely in Germany. With some careful planning and extra work Matt reactivated his high school French while learning German, and completed the IEP in 2001 with a BS in Ocean Engineering and a BA with majors in both French and German. The IEP learned from Matt to be flexible, to support students wanting to push the limits, and to let the program adapt to individual needs.

Having spent his fourth year abroad, completing a semester of intensive language study in France and a six-month internship with an SAP research team in Karlsruhe, Germany, Matt had become highly proficient in both languages and skilled at understanding other cultural perspectives and how engineers work in Europe. Matt also made the most of his engineering education, pursuing his interest in the oceans and the technical challenges put forward by a very specialized faculty in Ocean Engineering at URI. Intrigued by the research on sonar technology being conducted by Professor James Miller at that time, Matt signed on as a research assistant and took on a project which would exceed the normal demands of an undergraduate program and would likewise satisfy his own need to push the typical limits, thereby boosting his trust in himself and strengthening his emerging entrepreneurial spirit. Looking

113

back, Matt tells us that the overall URI and IEP experience provided him with personal growth on many sides, not the least of which was gaining the confidence to go it alone and start his own company.

Matt learned the essence of teamwork at URI, but through his internships he also learned to work independently. When at Brown & Sharpe for a summer internship, at SAP for his IEP internship abroad, or working for Professor Jim Miller, Matt was given challenges beyond anything he had done before, and asked to meet them independently. He accepted the challenge, more than made his way through successfully, and found his confidence and spirit of independence growing by leaps and bounds.

Matt is founder and Vice President for Engineering of FarSounder, Incorporated, a technology-leading company supplying the marine industry with three-dimensional sonar detection devices ensuring a far higher degree of navigational safety for ocean going vessels of all kinds. Beginning with his project work at URI, Matt came to realize that the currently available one- or two-dimensional sonar detection devices still leave ships very vulnerable, especially in unchartered waters or ocean areas subject to changing conditions. FarSounder's three-dimensional sonars scan with a 90 degree field of view and produce real-time 3D images, updated every two seconds, with enormous benefits for yachts navigating in shallow or unknown waters, commercial fishermen, passenger vessels, freighters and even war ships. His company has also developed a 360 degree system that can scan for the safety of ships, which could, for example, be threatened by terrorists while in port.

The founding and organization of FarSounder is an interesting story in and of itself. Matt came upon the basic idea and the foundations of the technology while an undergrad and was able to co-found the company together with Professor Jim Miller of URI who still sits on the company's board of directors. When graduating, Matt tells us that he had a choice either to take a job or to make his own job. The decision was made somewhat easier by the fact that his engineer mother who had already demonstrated success as a business leader, was ready to jump on board, bringing her management experience and ability to seek external funding. Though the company is still small, FarSounder has a unique technology with a growing reputation and customer base. They have received numerous federal grants and their technology is rapidly becoming increasingly promising for the marine industry and for Homeland Security. Matt's optimism is based in part on the fact that FarSounder products, when compared to those developed by or for the military, is far less complex, far more user friendly and reliable. Matt and his team have developed a technology which the big players have abandoned as impossible. He is thus confident today that there is no real competition.

We can understand how FarSounder is consonant with Matt's technical interests, but we might think that a small company in Warwick, Rhode Island might not be the place to use cross-cultural communication skills. Matt assures us, however, that his global skill set has been critical to the success of the company and plays a role almost daily. First of all, Matt's employees have always been very international, coming from Jamaica, Nepal, Russia, India, the UK, and the Ukraine. He is, therefore, using his cross-cultural appreciation on a daily basis in his own offices in Rhode Island. Secondly, and perhaps even more important, his customers are scattered across the globe. FarSounder has sold its products to customers in many countries, including France, Germany, Monaco, Spain, Portugal, Italy, Croatia, Turkey, Malta, China, the Netherlands, Nigeria, Australia, Singapore and Japan. He is in daily contact by e-mail or telephone with customers around the world, regularly uses French, sometimes German, but also Italian and Spanish, which he has learned on a conversational level for business purposes. FarSounder relies heavily on dealers in these countries, but Matt must travel regularly to help train technicians, install, or fine-tune products for customers. Trade shows are also important reasons for travel and the use of languages other than English. Matt has found that English is the most prevalent language for his business, but that the ability to speak the language of the customer is an enormous sales advantage. Also, he points out that English proficiency is very uneven from country to country and is often simply not enough for dealing even with the basics.

Matt is grateful to URI and the IEP for many things, but perhaps first on the list is the program of study that bolstered his ability to work and think independently and eventually believe he could found his own company at age 23. He gives a great deal of credit to his engineer parents, both of whom were entrepreneurs themselves, but he also attributes much of his confidence to the IEP which broadened his world view, expanded his mind in other directions, immersed him in other cultures and led him to work experiences through which he could learn to solve problems on his own. Certainly Matt had the necessary "raw materials" to succeed with or without the IEP, but as he says himself: *I believe the IEP enforced my belief that I can achieve great things and implement big ideas.*

The IEP is proud of Matt as an alum who represents the program's goals of bridging the disciplines at the university, but also through life-long pursuits. In addition to practicing this ideal in his career, he does this as well by maintaining his commitment to the community as an artist. Matt is an enthusiastic participant and contributor to an organization in Providence, Rhode Island known as AS220, which, among other things, explores the intersection of cutting-edge technology with the realm of artistic expression. Here he is able to teach courses related to the goals of AS220, but also to create works of art using devices and instruments such as laser cutting machinery.

What can we learn from Matthew Zimmerman?
1. From Matt the IEP learned to be more flexible and creative on behalf of the individual student. While we envisioned students learning French, German **or** Spanish along with engineering, Matt decided that he could learn German **and** French, and to have international experiences in two countries. While I had

some fears of diluting his focus, Matt built upon the French he had learned in school and then spent six months in both France and Germany, mastering each language well. Looking back, and considering his language and culture needs today, he certainly made the right choice. Since Matt's years at URI, we have regularly encouraged students to set trilingualism as their goal, which is, after all, a normal expectation for students from other parts of the world.

2. Matt is among those former students who have helped us to recognize the degree to which multi-lingualism and experiences abroad build personal confidence and independence. When thinking in terms of assessment, academics reach first for those things which are measureable and therefore more tangible. The most straight-forward product of the IEP is language acquisition which can be evaluated before and after by standardized proficiency guide-lines, e.g., the oral proficiency exams of the American Council on the Teaching of Foreign Languages (ACTFL). Other tools are available to measure gains in cross-cultural communication, even if in their infancy. What we do not measure, however, are so-called soft skills such as the ability to deal with ambiguity, the ability to adapt to new environments, the ability to deal with other cultural perspectives, the ability to problem solve independently, and gains in self confidence. Matt tells us that he gained a great deal in these areas as a result of living, studying and working abroad and that the IEP helped him to have the courage to found his own company.

3. *Think Big We Do* is the slogan used to market the University of Rhode Island, and we are told by the persons who developed this concept that the IEP was one of the university programs leading to its choice. Had they interviewed Matt Zimmerman, he too could have been such an inspiration. The IEP tells students to master a language with a full major, not just to take a few classes. It tells students not to just

117

travel or spend a few weeks abroad, but to spend a full year in culturally immersed study and work. It tells the university that academics themselves must dare to be entrepreneurial in their programming. And Matt tells us to learn two languages rather than one, and to dare to take the results of one's research and dreams to the marketplace, indeed to dare to be entrepreneurial.

4. Matt too, along with others in this volume, helps us to see the degree to which international education affects one's life at both the professional and personal levels. Given his yearning for travel, his love of language, his experiences abroad through the IEP, it is not surprising that his wife, Katie, was an honors degree French student and a high school French teacher, who also spent more than a year abroad.

5. Matt's experience with language learning also mirrors that of several other students in this study. Though he had taken French from grade 6 through grade 11, he believes that he learned very little, largely because he "simply did not care" (his own words) and saw no real value in speaking another language. This attitude changed through his high school trip to Russia, and then took on new meaning when he realized that learning German at URI would enable him to go to Germany and do research with a high-level team at one of the world's leading software developers. If we wish to have more students in the language classroom, the language learning process must be related to the students' primary interests and must hold out the promise of personal benefit other than vague qualities such as "expanding one's horizons."

For Matt Zimmerman, a Global Engineer: *has the skills and ability to frequently work on projects with customers in other countries and coordinate work with their foreign technical staff.*

118

Nika McManus

The IEP has given me exceptional opportunities, and extreme flexibility in choices for professional direction, growth, and expansion in the technical, global, and linguistic areas. It has broadened my view of different cultures within, and outside, the workplace. It taught me to be flexible, and able to adjust to new environments, and new opportunities. Quickly.

Born: Moscow, Russia
Citizenship: USA
High School: Cumberland, Rhode Island
IEP Degrees: BA in German; BS in Mechanical Engineering, 2002
Graduate Degrees: University of Rhode Island, Masters of Science in Mechanical Engineering, Technical University of Braunschweig, *Diplom-Ingenieurin,* Dual Degree Program, *2007*
Current position: Structural Analysis Engineer, Boeing Corporation
Past Position: Technical Support Engineer, Vision Systems, Inc., Hingham, Massachusetts

If one ever doubts the importance or relevance of a quality engineering education, one need only consider the catastrophic accident of the Space Shuttle Columbia in 2003, or the technical challenges of developing the 787 Dreamliner. And if one ever doubts the importance of a global and comprehensive understanding of issues such as this, one need only study the education and career of IEP graduate Nika McManus, who is a member of the Boeing Corporation's Advanced Structural Analysis Group.

One could easily think that a company like Boeing must be as American as a company can possibly be, even if it sells its products across the globe. While Boeing is indeed a symbol for American technical and corporate leadership, it is simultaneously as global as a company can possibly be. Consider the new Boeing 787 Dreamliner, which is assembled in the USA, but consists of components designed and produced in approximately 40 countries throughout the world. Boeing understands that the best airliner in the world requires the best expertise and the best talent, and that in this era of globalization these are not necessarily found exclusively in the United States. To maintain industry leadership, Boeing needs to know the competition in Europe (Airbus), Brazil (Embraer), or in emerging economies such as China and India, and it must maintain relationships with and have access to the best people and the latest developments everywhere. Boeing simply cannot operate in a national vacuum, if it wants to maintain its top position in one of the world's biggest industries. For that reason, their corporate technical teams must, by definition, be international; and for that reason Boeing's engineers must include team members with international experience and global communication skills – like the IEP graduate Nika McManus.

Nika McManus has an extraordinary background. Fluent in English, Russian, and German, she holds the B.S. in Mechanical Engineering, the B.A. in German, and dual degrees at the master's level (M.S. and *Diplom*) from the University of Rhode Island and its partner in Germany, the Technische Universität Braunschweig. Having completed her master's thesis in Germany at Braunschweig's Institute of Aircraft Design and Lightweight Structures, she was a natural for the aerospace industry, and thus works today in Boeing's Advanced Structural Analysis Group with a focus on structural design, optimization, ballistic vulnerability, shock, impact, and advanced dynamic components. This team of approximately thirty engineers is based in the Philadelphia area, and serves the needs of all Boeing branches, as well as other customers from around the world, who seek their expertise. It is not surprising that such a team, which might deal with Space Shuttle issues one day, 787 Dreamliner design the next day, and then with the problems faced by an aerospace company in Korea the next, is itself very international, made up of global engineers like Nika, who have in-depth international knowledge, and experience and/or who are themselves originally from other countries, such as Russia, Italy, Japan, China, or India.

Nika was born and raised in Moscow until the age of 15, when her professional pianist mother married an American and moved with Nika to Cumberland, Rhode Island. Coming from one of the world's largest cities, Moscow, and having been raised as a child under a totalitarian regime, the change to small-town USA must have been a significant culture shock at the beginning. Nika was put under pressure to learn English rapidly and to adapt swiftly to a new and very different lifestyle. But, intelligent as she is, she did so with relative ease, learning English quickly and graduating from Cumberland High School on schedule. Part of her success in school may be attributed to her early education in Russia, where the standards are higher in math and science, enabling her to ease into the American curriculum while perfecting her English. Having established a stellar record in these subjects in high school, it is perhaps not surprising that she chose engineering as her major when accepted for admission to the University of Rhode Island.

Nika did not join the IEP in her freshman year at URI, but she was definitely intrigued by the idea, and jumped into the German IEP with a full commitment in her second year, after proving to herself that she would be able to handle the university workload and establish a good grade point average. Not only was she interested in doing part of her studies in Europe, where she knew she would feel at home and could take courses not available at URI, but she was also inspired to learn German by a family secret which had come to light in the wake of the fall of the Soviet Union, namely, that her grandfather was German. Now that this fact no longer needed to be hidden from the authorities, she was excited about the idea of learning the language and living in the original culture of her grandparents. Nika's grandfather is still living in Moscow. She visits him periodically and is proud to be able to converse with him in his native tongue, and he with her.

Nika was an enthusiastic IEP undergrad, committed to learning German, happy to be associated with a program that valued international background and multilingualism. She made up for the fact that she did not begin German as a freshman by attending URI's summer immersion program in German, the German Summer School of the Atlantic. In other available summers, the program helped her secure internship experiences with global companies in Rhode Island, where she gained her first real-life exposure to her field. Successful in her studies in both German and mechanical engineering, she spent her fourth year in Germany, studying in the fall in Braunschweig, and then interning for the commercial vehicle headquarters of Volkswagen AG in the city of Hannover.

Nika speaks fondly of her year in Germany, which turned out to be positive enough for her to want to return for her masters program. She was enamored by the German university structure, with its wealth of facilities and its high-level research institutes. In addition to her coursework in German and engineering, she also used her semester in Braunschweig to cultivate her broader interests by taking courses in three-dimensional modeling at the city's cooperating art institute, *Die Hochschule für Bildende Künste Braunschweig* (HBK Braunschweig). Being already in Europe, she was also able to spend Christmas vacation with her grandfather in Moscow.

Nika had a vey good experience interning at the VW

plant in nearby Hanover where the vans and commercial vehicles are built. She was put to work with the teams responsible for the latest assembly line modifications, making it possible to build more than one vehicle model on a single line. Specifically, her group had to decide how to integrate the installation of differing fuel tanks into this process and whether to do so manually or by robot. This experience helped Nika make good progress culturally, and linguistically; and technically she learned to appreciate what it means to work in a team and to value the attention to detail and quality, for which German engineering is famous.

Following her graduation in 2002, Nika went to work as a Technical Support Engineer for Vision Systems, Inc. in Hingham, Massachusetts - a company manufacturing and selling video-based surveillance and security products. In this position she provided online and telephone technical support for North American customers, and marketing and product managers. In addition, she performed hands-on repairs, and prepared online video demonstrations. Though her first job gave her experience and a decent salary, it did not satisfy her long-term goals, and she felt the need for greater intellectual stimulation and more education. She also was very open to the ideas of going back to Europe.

When Nika stopped by my office during this time period to explore other opportunities, and to seek my advice, I urged her to consider the newly developed Dual Degree Masters Program in conjunction with our partner university in Germany, the Technical University of Braunschweig. This would enable her to study for one year at URI, taking master's-level courses, and gaining exposure to thesis-related research, and then to spend the second year in Germany, again taking master's-level courses and completing her thesis there, overseen by faculty from both institutions. Fortunately, I was able to offer her financial support through a grant I held at that time from the German Ministry of Economics. Nika immediately declared that this was for her. Like Eric Sargent, who is also described in this volume, she was not deterred by the fact that the program was new and that she would, to an extent, serve as a guinea pig.

Nika joined the Dual Degree Masters Program in the Fall of 2004 with a passion. She took both a full load of graduate courses in mechanical engineering, and also committed to a research assistantship with Professor David Taggart, whose work in the areas of computation mechanics, numerical finite element based topological optimization schemes, and finite element implementation of cardiac tissue enabled Nika to focus on computational research, with applications in structural optimization, bone remodeling, and nature adaptation theories, as well as tissue mechanics. She did not consider at the time that this work could also apply directly to non-human structural issues, and that her thesis in Braunschweig would evolve later to focus on aircraft structures.

Nika left for Braunschweig after the 2004-2005 academic year to spend the second year at our partner university, where her studies were ultimately extended for a third year. First, the course requirements there were more than originally anticipated, and it also took Nika a lengthy period of time to decide where and with whom to do her research. Overwhelmed at first by the organizational structure of a German university, which consists of well over 100 very independent research institutes, she decided ultimately to transition from nature adaptation theories to aircraft structures, while maintaining an emphasis on computational analysis. She first did a special research project on the relationship between bone and aircraft remodeling techniques, before applying her expertise in the Finite Element Analysis of a highly complex part segment between the C56-6 and C57-4 frames of the Airbus A340-600 for her thesis.

Nika felt very much at home in Germany and loved the working environment of the Institute of Aircraft Design and Lightweight Structures, where she worked under the guidance of Professor Peter Horst, and ultimately graduated with the prestigious German title of *Diplom-Ingenieurin*. During her time in Braunschweig, she learned not only to work with the thoroughness and attention to detail of German engineering, but also gained exposure to aerospace engineering from the European perspective. Combining this with the practicality and matter-of-factness of the American approach and the URI expertise in Finite Element Analysis, Nika had become an extraordinarily competent engineer, with highly advanced skills, thus making her very attractive for a unit such as the Boeing Advanced Structural Analysis Group.

Nika is happy with her position at Boeing, which is both technically challenging, and calls upon her global skills. As mentioned above, her team comprises a group for whom international is a given, and for whom it is routine to be working with and for others from around the world. As a result, if there is a meeting with a group from Russia or Germany, it is understood that Nika will be there to ensure there are no language or cultural miscommunications. Likewise, she holds the expertise for translating documents, drawings, e-mails, letters, and contracts arriving in these languages. Although she has not been called upon to travel, or be assigned short- or long-term to these countries, that is possible at any time. With so many Boeing locations, and so many customers, and suppliers around the globe, it is inevitable, that her services will be required out of country.

What can we learn from Nika McManus?

1. As we have seen with so many of the cases in this study, the IEP attracts, and encourages young people willing to go the extra mile, and willing to take calculated risks. In a sense, the IEP curriculum itself is a risk, requiring students to invest in language and culture study over, and against pure technology courses. Furthermore, it requires extra time, delaying entry to the job market, and sending students considerably outside of their comfort zones.

    Nika McManus not only opted for all of these things as an undergrad, but then gave up a salaried position to enter the Dual Degree Masters Program, which was at that time highly experimental and fraught with unanswered questions. She went to Braunschweig without knowing exactly how many courses she would have to take, without being sure, that her German was strong enough for the tasks, and without knowing the precise nature of her thesis or who her advisor would be.

We have seen repeatedly in this study that the IEP students are willing to take risks when major benefits can accrue, and that the program nurtures and encourages this quality as a requisite skill for the global workplace. We have also seen, for example, in the cases of Sharon Ruggieri, Matt Zimmerman, Ana Franco, Jesse Schneider, and others, that risk taking is strongly tied to dreaming big, and to being open to unforeseen opportunities which would not be there otherwise. And this is certainly the case for Nika McManus.

2. We can learn from Nika, as well as from several others in this study, that the IEP, and programs like the IEP, are magnets not only for bright, and motivated students, but for what some would call right-brained/left-brained individuals. It is a given that the IEP students will have to be able to excel in math and physics. But a high percentage of IEP students also are good communicators, with multiple interests and multiple skills. They were high school students with academic strengths in several areas and could have chosen to go in many directions. Nika is an artist, and an athlete; she dances competitively, runs, plays the piano at an advanced level, she snowboards, does ballet, is a certified cycling instructor, and also rides. And, as with her engineering, she is driven to excel in all of these things. If one considers the multiple interests of so many of the students in this study (Matt Zimmerman as a musician, an artist, and a scuba diver; Ana Franco as a triathlon competitor, Sharon Ruggieri is active in the martial arts; John DiMuro sings chorally, plays the piano, follows world affairs closely, and is

always active in his community; many travel regularly to new countries, and engage in language learning), it is easy to conclude, that the IEP, with its requisite challenges, represents a magnet for young people who can do it all. It is safe to conclude, that the IEP is attractive for them, in part, because it allows, and encourages them to continue to pursue their varied interests.

3. From Nika we also learn once again the importance of personal outreach to students and the value of mentoring and advising. When she came to my office as a first year student, inquiring about the IEP, I understood, that she was a natural for the program, but also, as an immigrant, uncertain, and lacking in confidence. My staff and I were willing to spend time with her to map out an academic plan, both as an undergrad, and then later as a graduate student. She knew we were there for her and that this would be a big factor for her to remain with the program. When asking students to take on a significant challenge, and to step out of their comfort zones, educators and their institutions need to be prepared to provide the necessary infrastructure for support and mentorship.

4. As I think of Nika's case as a student in our evolving Dual Degree Masters Program, I am reminded of the need for faculty such as myself to be persistent on behalf of our students. Students in such programs need to be independent, self-confident, risk-taking, and persistent themselves. Since such programs bump up against so many well-established rules and traditions of the academy, we ourselves need to bear witness to the qualities we advocate. We need to be there for our students when the system is pushing unfairly against their progress.

For Nika McManus: *A Global Engineer has unique characteristics, combining a technical foundation and fluency in multiple languages with global team and cultural*

127

strengths. Characteristics include: flexibility, ability to adjust, to learn new techniques quickly and efficiently, and to work, and deliver with a team.

Sareh Rajaee

The IEP experience, especially my year abroad, helped me build confidence in my interpersonal communication skills, in my critical thinking skills, and in myself as an individual. The IEP showed me what I am capable of, and I am now a stronger, happier, and more independent person because of it.

The combination of critical thinking from the engineering background and cross-cultural communication from the international background gave me a unique skill set that will be especially helpful in making me a better physician.

Age: 27
Born: in Iran
Citizenship: USA
High School: East Greenwich, Rhode Island
IEP Degrees: BA in German; BS in Biomedical Engineering, 2006
Graduate Degrees: M.D., Alpert Medical School, Brown University, May 2011; Master's in Public Health, Harvard School of Public Health, Harvard University, May 2011
Current Position: Residency in Vascular Surgery, Yale New Haven Hospital, Yale University, New Haven, Connecticut

Beginning IEP students often express uncertainty and even anxiety about careers in engineering. Some suffer from preconceived images of isolated lives spent in a cubicle in front of a computer; others are studying engineering at their parents' urging and simply have little idea of what their course of study is or will mean, and are anxious as a result. My advice has always been to stay the course with their rigorous and solid program of technical and international study and let things unfold one step at a time. I have done my best to assure that the IEP will most certainly enable them to choose from a variety of career paths. Engineering itself yields almost unlimited opportunities, some of which are directly related to technical research and innovation, while others are more related to fields such as business or law. Given the rapid pace of change in the world of technology, it is even safe to say that there will be careers for engineers in the coming years which have yet to be imagined. The crux of my advice is that engineering, especially when combined with the in-depth experience of another language and culture, will open doors and change lives, but only for those who stay the course.

Like many others, Sareh Rajaee did not know at the beginning of her studies if she wanted to be an engineer.

But, wisely, she stayed with the program, which, in her case, became a powerful starting point for a career in medicine and public health. Sareh chose the IEP because of its challenging nature, her desire to prove her academic abilities to herself and others, and her wish to be competitive if and when applying for graduate study. She also chose the IEP for its international orientation and her eagerness to expose herself to other cultural values and other languages along the way to whatever her career might be. She quickly found the program to be a way to pursue her interests and, at the same time, to demonstrate her abilities and her eagerness to go the extra mile. Sareh opted for the German IEP in order to learn a fourth language (she already knew English, Farsi, and French) and to be able to spend time abroad. And with medicine already in the back of her mind, she chose biomedical engineering as her technical field. Sareh's instincts were right that a challenging combination of studies would serve her well. Already in her Junior year, she was able to secure acceptance to the Brown University Medical School Early Identification Program where she has since completed her M.D. Typical of Sareh's commitment to going the extra mile, she also enrolled in the Masters of Public Health Program at Harvard University where she simultaneously completed that degree along side her Brown M.D.

One might find it a stretch to include Sareh in this study, since our goal is to determine to what extent the IEP education has made a difference in global engineering careers. One might indeed argue that Sareh left engineering for a different career direction for which her technical background, her acquisition of German and time spent abroad were hardly necessary. Indeed, her field today is medicine and she will rarely need to speak German in American hospitals. But, we need to look more closely at the relationship between these fields and experiences, for Sareh tells us herself that she still considers herself to be an engineer and, indeed, owes much of her success in medical school to the IEP!

Is medicine engineering? Is engineering medicine? Certainly we live in an era when disciplines and professions all seem to intersect and support one another, and that is most definitely true of engineering and medicine. When one considers the mechanisms used in the treatment of disease today, such as artificial joints, valves, muscles, and organs, or the degree to which computers and electronics are applied to the human body in robotic limbs, heart-related devices, through medicinal chemistry, or even the many roles of technology in diagnosis or in the operating room, it is clear that engineering is playing a greater and greater role in health care. Engineering may not be medicine per se, but medicine certainly can no longer exist without engineering.

Sareh did not feel that she was abandoning engineering when she decided to go to medical school; nor does she feel today, five years after graduation from URI, that she is no longer an engineer. She feels, rather, that she has built upon her undergraduate skills and has specialized in such a way as to be able to apply those skills to the human physiology. Sareh was right that the IEP would help her to sell herself as an excellent student, a person ready to go the extra mile, and a strong candidate for medical school. She even found her IEP background as an item of great interest and value when interviewing for residency positions at places such as Yale. At the same time, she feels that she is applying her engineering skills on a daily basis, which include a way of thinking and a valuable set of problem-solving skills. Sareh explains that in this way: *I feel that the human body is in many ways a very sophisticated and complicated machine. As a doctor, and in particular, as a future surgeon, I am also still in many ways a Biomedical Engineer. It just so happens that in this case, every machine can be quite unique, and there is constantly more to be discovered. For example, cardiovascular medicine is all about pumps, valves, and fluid mechanics, so when assessing patients with cardiovascular disease, I do find that I have an easier time determining their differential diagnosis as well as plan of action for treatment because of what I learned during my undergraduate experience in engineer-*

ing. I also use devices that were developed by biomedical engineers, such as Doppler ultrasound machines and electrocardiograms. Having built a portable EKG machine myself during my biomedical engineering senior design course under the guidance of Dr. Ying Sun, I feel that I am now able to better interpret EKGs because I know how the devices function.

Is medicine a global field and profession? Is international experience important preparation for physicians? Aside from the fact that research and development in the medical fields has become a global phenomenon (consider, for example, the role that Germany and Siemens play in the evolution of devices such as MRI machines), the very practice of medicine occurs in a much more diverse and multicultural setting than in the past. Sareh rarely has the chance to use her German, French or Farsi, yet she tells us that her cross-cultural communication skills acquired through the IEP are put to use each day. American hospitals, especially in urban settings, are filled with staff, professionals, and patients deriving from a multiplicity of ethnic, cultural, and national backgrounds. In our modern world, disease itself has become a global phenomenon, demanding a far greater awareness of the world than in the past. Sareh argues that her undergraduate years gave her a tremendous advantage over her colleagues, most of whom have never lived, studied, or worked abroad. Sareh furthermore plans to take all of her skills with her in the coming years as a volunteer physician and surgeon in developing countries with great need.

Sareh was born in Iran and came to this country at the age of two, when her father was admitted to a graduate program in mechanical engineering. Not untypically, the Rajaee family stayed in the U.S. and she grew up in Rhode Island, attending public school and graduating from East Greenwich High School. Sareh attributes much of her drive for excellence and her eagerness to go the extra mile to her parents and to the immigrant attitude that one must work extra hard to succeed in this new homeland. She has at times struggled with and resisted the pressure from her parents who want to see Sareh achieve her best, but she has never let them down and she does not in the least regret where her hard work has taken her.

Much of Sareh's openness to other cultures and languages stems from her heritage and upbringing. She was raised in a Farsi-speaking family and periodically had the opportunity to spend time in Iran. When she learned about the IEP, therefore, and the chance to learn a new language and spend a full-year as a student and intern in Europe, she did not give it a second thought. This would be her chance to travel, to get to know a new area of the world, to be on her own for the first time, to advance professionally and distinguish herself as an applicant for additional opportunities, such as medical school. In short, the IEP offered her what she wanted and needed to be able to make engineering something special and to make the University of Rhode Island the right choice for her undergraduate degree(s).

Sareh was fully engaged in IEP life as an undergraduate. She associated closely with other IEP students, many of whom have become life-long friends, and lived and participated fully in the residential IEP House living and learning community. She also engaged fully with the newly emerging biomedical engineering program, and interned both on and off campus. She was, for example, a URI Biomedical Engineering Assistant from June 2003- August 2004, when she helped to develop an assistive technology device to be used at Rhode Island's Slater Hospital by patients with disabilities. While abroad in Germany during her fourth year of the IEP, she interned at AVISO GmbH Mechatronic Systems in Greiz, Germany from January 2005 to August 2005. There she conducted beta testing for the Cellcelector™, a multifunctional robot system for automatically isolating and separating cell clones and individual cells. In the summer of 2006, she worked at the Department of Medical Pharmacology and Physiology at the University of Missouri in Columbia, Missouri. Supported by the Research Experience for Undergraduates (REU), sponsored by the National Science Foundation (NSF), she developed a computer model using Microsoft Excel and Visual Basic Editor to simulate sodium pump production, trafficking, degradation, and removal, in order to determine the time-effectiveness of selective versus random sodium pump removal.

Sareh was not originally on the list of IEP alums for this study, mainly because she is still quite young and has not actually been in the global workplace since leaving URI. Midway through this project, however, I received an e-mail from Sareh updating me on her status: May 2011 graduation from Brown's medical school, simultaneous graduation from the Harvard School of Public Health, and acceptance to the Yale residency in vascular surgery. While sharing this news with me, she wrote: "and I owe it all to the IEP." Certainly this had to be an exaggeration to make her former director feel good in retirement. And yet, when I pursued this issue with her, it is clear that the IEP gave her what she needed at that point in her life. Not unlike many of the others in this study, the overall experience of pursuing a liberal arts degree along with a technical degree gave her greater breadth of skill and understanding. As she tells us, however, being able to spend a year abroad, in a new language, immersed in another culture, enabled her to grow personally and to gain the inner confidence and strength to take on problems and challenges which heretofore had seemed simply over-whelming. In her words: *I feel that the experience of learning how to live and work on my own in a foreign country really helped me to be more courageous in my future career pursuits. I became more fearless about taking on new opportunities such as completing additional internships and research projects.*

What can we learn from Sareh Rajaee?
1. From Sareh we learn first of all the value of the IEP as a foundation for many careers, some of which may be more or less obviously related to the engineering classroom. Sareh gained important academic knowledge as an engineer, which applies directly to her medical career, but she also learned ways of

thinking from the IEP, both technically and cross-culturally, which have served her well. As she tells us: *I feel that the combination of critical thinking from the engineering background and cross-cultural communication from the international background have given me a unique skill set that will be especially helpful in making me a better physician.*

2. From a purely pragmatic point of view, we also learn from Sareh the extent to which the IEP is a powerful "resume-builder," and a good undergraduate starting point for students planning to apply for very competitive graduate programs. *I was attracted to the IEP because I knew I wanted to enhance my undergraduate education with an enriching experience that would make me stand out in my future applications.* This strategy, which worked well for Sareh, has also proven itself with other IEPers who have gone to graduate programs at MIT, Princeton, and other first-class institutions and/or to fast-track career trainee programs at major corporations.

3. As is the case for most persons in this study, we also learn from Sareh the value of extended study abroad as a tool for building self-confidence. Sareh describes herself as a shy and sometimes less confident person, who did not find it easy to declare her independence from home. She is clear that her year spent in Germany made an enormous difference for her, where she was taken out of the "spoon-fed" American higher education model and expected to make daily decisions on her own, regarding academic life, personal choice, housing, meals, and so on. *The IEP showed me what I am capable of, and I am now a stronger, happier, and more independent person because of it.*

4. Sareh's case is also a powerful reminder of the role that cross-cultural communication can and must play within our own home institutions, such as hospitals. Having been exposed to cultural differences between the U.S., Germany, and the Middle East, Sareh is in

a unique situation to tolerate, understand, and bridge differences affecting both staff-to-staff and doctor-to-patient communication. She is in a position to not only tolerate, but to appreciate and value difference as it impacts some of the most intense moments of life and death in our ever increasingly multicultural society.

Sareh defines the global engineer in this way, pointing out that the concept goes far beyond simple travel and may be practiced at home as well as abroad: *A global engineer or doctor is someone who is capable of both cross-cultural communication and cross-cultural sensitivity. I don't think going abroad is necessarily what makes a global engineer or doctor. For example, one can work in the United States with refugee or immigrant populations and still be considered a "global" doctor. In contrast, simply going abroad does not make one a "global" anything. For example, if an engineer has to go to the Chinese headquarters of his company for training but makes no effort to communicate with or learn about Chinese people and culture, then by no means is he a "global engineer."*

Ryan Cournoyer

Ryan Cournoyer (right) having lunch with clients
in Izmir, Turkey – before his next flight.

*Most American employees from Bentley were never given
the opportunity to work overseas. I was given that
opportunity within three years of my start. This would not
have happened without my schooling in the IEP program.*

Age: 30
High School: Enfield, Connecticut
IEP Degrees: BA in French; BS in Civil Engineering,
2004
Current position: Sales Engineer, Wescor Associates,
Wrentham, Massachusetts.
Past Position(s): Technical support analyst, Applications Engineer, Sales Manager, Bentley Systems
Incorporated, Exton, Pennsylvania

Ryan Cournoyer is the son of hard working immigrants to this country from French-speaking Canada, and one of the first in his family to seek a higher education degree. Like many offspring of recently arrived families, he did not know that the language spoken in his home could serve him well as an engineer in the United States. For that reason, he had spent six years in school learning Spanish rather than French. When visiting universities and exploring his options, however, he discovered that he could study his family's native language along with civil engineering at URI and perhaps even complete an internship in his parents' homeland. Still unaware that such a decision would open excellent career opportunities, this familial heritage consideration became the deciding factor and differentiator for choosing URI as his undergraduate school.

Today Ryan is an expert in water management systems and especially the computer software programs that enable municipalities and the private sector to map, plan, manage, optimize, replace, and coordinate water, wastewater, and storm drainage systems. Ryan developed this expertise through his studies at URI, and then through his international work as a software and systems manager at Bentley Systems, Incorporated, one of the world's leading companies for the management of large infrastructure systems. After six years at Bentley, Ryan now applies his skills and knowledge as a key team member of a small consulting company which makes its services and expertise available to municipalities in the New England area for the design, construction, and management of wastewater treatment plants.

Laypersons might not consider tap water, wastewater or storm drain water to be associated with global business and technology; yet Ryan Cournoyer's career path has proven that they most certainly are. This is especially so today when water is increasingly recognized as a precious resource which must be carefully conserved and managed to meet the needs of the world's growing population in a time of alarming climate change. Because Bentley Systems works with this in mind and consciously seeks the best technology across the globe for applications both at home and abroad, a civil engineer like Ryan with a second language and global skills was very attractive as a new hire in 2004.

Ryan joined the water management division of Bentley Systems (the company also deals with roadways, bridges, railways, power plants and other infrastructure components) upon graduation from the IEP and quickly discovered that his French language and culture skills would be to his advantage. When trained in sales, development, and management of Bentley's software for hydraulic modeling, it was not surprising that Quebec became a major part of his area of responsibility. Very quickly his French was used on a daily basis with customers who welcomed the fact that their Bentley representative was not only an expert in water systems, but also fluent in their tongue and familiar with their culture and heritage. Being the son of a French-Canadian family made him a natural for that position, and he was quickly promoted to serve as the liaison between the U.S. and Quebec offices of the company.

But Canada was by no means the limit of Ryan's international exposure while working for Bentley. Because of his French and his overall global competency resulting from his study of language and culture and his time spent abroad, he was also given responsibility for hydraulic modeling software sales in Belgium, France, Morocco, Tunisia, Jordan, Israel, and South Africa. At Bentley he travelled frequently and was given tasks that are seldom enjoyed by young engineers in a company of this size. He was assigned to headquarters in Holland for six months in 2007, and travelled for Bentley in Turkey, Greece, Romania, Egypt, and Iceland. While most American engineers were not entrusted with work abroad, he had regular assignments around the world after just three years with the company, and even managed a group of engineers in Europe for a period of time. As he tells us, *this would not have happened without my schooling in the IEP program.*

Ryan (right) at dinner with engineers in Greece

In each of the positions I held at Bentley, there was an aspect of international support and sales. I would not have been offered my position in Europe for 2007 had I not had the IEP.

Ryan left Bentley Systems in 2011 to join a very young and small company focusing on the planning, building, and management of wastewater treatment plants in the New England area. As he explains, his work with Bentley was very focused on modeling with a highly specialized software. His work was very rewarding in the short term, but had limited potential for the broader responsibilities and professional advancement and rewards that he sought in the longer term. Going with a small company certainly brought career risks which he would not have known if he had stayed at Bentley Systems, but, like many IEP grads, he was willing to take a calculated risk if there was a reasonable potential for success and growth. In his new position, he is one of four very committed, entrepreneurial, and enthusiastic young engineers.

It would be easy to assume that leaving a global giant like Bentley and joining a small company serving New

England municipalities would not call upon the international skills which had become such an important part of his life. Ryan tells us, however, that even though his customers are strictly Americans, his knowledge of wastewater treatment systems worldwide sets him apart from the competition. As a result of his extensive professional reach, he is very familiar with the technology available to his business across the globe and thus brings a very international network of suppliers to the table. In short, when designing and/or bidding a wastewater treatment plant for a customer, he is in almost daily contact with partners around the world, purchasing some components from Germany, others from Korea, and so forth. In his words: *My IEP education and the international experience I gained from Bentley are huge assets when conversing with and working with our partners. There is something to be said about being an American with business and work experience outside of the country that separates an engineer from the rest.* Had Ryan not worked internationally for several years, he would have little knowledge of the industry practices from those parts of the world, which are so different and often more advanced and which he can now bring to customers in New England.

Ryan is personally very satisfied with the course of his professional career to date, which he attributes in large part to his overall engineering and language/culture education, but also to the values and heritage of his family. The son of 1970 immigrants to the United States from Quebec, Canada, he was not born into a highly educated family, but nevertheless, a family knowing the importance of education, discipline and hard work. Arriving in Connecticut with almost nothing, his parents established a residential and commercial construction company and quickly built a reputation for quality and dependability. Like so many immigrants, it was their dream that their children would do their best and reach a level of professional and personal success unavailable to them. Ryan grew up in this environment and was thus naturally encouraged to work hard in school and plan to attend a university. Since he excelled in math and science and since he grew up in an environment of construction and design, civil engineering would be a natural course for him. As mentioned above, when he learned that he could study that field at URI and combine it with the study of his parents' native language and heritage, selecting URI as his university became a simple decision.

When approaching his fourth year of the IEP and making plans to study and work abroad, Ryan asked if it would not be possible to complete this part of the program in Quebec rather than in Europe. The IEP agreed that it would make sense for him to do this, i.e., to immerse himself in the culture of his family heritage, where he could, among other things, spend time with French-speaking relatives. Rather than studying and interning, Ryan was able to complete a research project with a faculty group at the IEP's partner school, the Université Laval, in Quebec City, Quebec. Here he was able to do research on the recovery from the Deluge du Saguenay flooding catastrophe and co-publish a paper with Laval faculty at the school's Hydraulic Institute.

Ryan was enthusiastic about his time spent in Quebec and found the experience to be eye-opening and the key to his being able to work for a company like Bentley upon graduation. As he tells us, *the IEP allows average Americans to look outside our country's borders and familiarize ourselves with the rest of the world, which is a must in order to conduct business in today's market and economy. When you have knowledge of another language or culture it is always looked upon favorably by international offices or employers. With Bentley having an international headquarters in Hoofddorp, Netherlands, the door was opened for me to work directly with them in Canada and Europe because I had the French skills and the cultural exposure.*

What can we learn from Ryan Cournoyer?
1. Ryan's case highlights the demand for IEP students in the global workplace and the potential for IEP alums to move rapidly up the career ladder because

of their global competency. Bentley Systems clearly needs engineers with global skills, but also clearly has difficulty finding them. Ryan was recognized for going the extra mile as an IEP student and was quickly rewarded with overseas responsibilities and advancements that were unavailable to other engineers, most of whom were still without a passport. The lessons learned from Ryan's case need to be shared at the high school level with students planning for engineering careers.

2. Ryan's case also demonstrates the extent of the globalization of today's workplace. While it is unlikely that we would consider the water from our taps, or the wastewater going down our drains as products associated with global technology, he proves to us that they certainly are. If we as a nation hope to compete in the long run, our infrastructure systems must meet a global standard, and our systems and equipment must be at least as good as those in other parts of the world. Similarly if we are to work together with other first-tier nations to stave off water shortages or quality issues at home and help those nations struggling for their most basic water needs, then we must be cooperating globally and we must be willing to both share our knowledge, but also be willing and able to learn from others. For this reason, more young professionals must have the global communication skills we see in Ryan Cournoyer. Even our wastewater engineers must be in regular contact with peers around the world.

3. Ryan also demonstrates the personal confidence that can come from having the courage to immerse oneself in a different culture and language. After having lived and worked in French-speaking Quebec, being assigned to Quebec by Bentley and being asked to serve as a liaison between the offices in the two countries was not as intimidating as it might be otherwise for a junior engineer in a large company. Likewise, his global skill set allowed him

to assume a leadership and supervisory position for projects in Europe and to travel for the company throughout, Europe, the Middle and Far East, and to Africa.

4. Ryan's case also bolsters the argument that in-depth exposure to one language and culture allows one to develop cross-cultural communication skills which are transferable to other areas of the world where one might have no prior experience. In his situation, living and working in Quebec enabled him to experience other cultural perspectives, both personal and professional, and to become sensitive to and tolerant of the points of views of others. The skills he used to work with engineers in Canada gave him a great advantage when then sent to Luxembourg, France, Belgium, and the Netherlands. But he found his abilities to interact with partners in those countries also applicable when sent to less familiar parts of the world, such as the Middle East, the Far East, and Africa.

5. Ryan stresses the importance and value of a liberal arts education along side his engineering training. He argues that companies seek engineers with breadth beyond the purely technical. The IEP, he believes, gave him exposure to language, literature, and culture, but also to students outside of the College of Engineering, and thus to a wider range of issues and interests. In his opinion, the program had numerous advantages, among them being an ability to communicate more effectively, both verbally and in writing, and a greater openness to other points of view.

6. Ryan also points out that the IEP enabled him to prove his willingness to separate himself from others, which is critical when searching for that first job. As he tells us: *In today's job market, job applications need every advantage possible to make a CV stand out from the rest. The tag team approach of the IEP (engineering with language and culture)*

provides every IEP grad that critical advantage.

Ryan defines the global engineer as: *an engineer who thinks outside of his / her local environment and is willing to contribute to the engineering community worldwide.*

Peter Alberg

Age: 42
High School: Pawtucket, Rhode Island
IEP Degrees: BS in Mechanical Engineering; BA in German, 1998
Current position: Sr. Design Engineer for Hilti GmbH, Kaufering, Germany
Past Positions: Engineer for Gabriele Design Group, East Greenwich, RI; Jr. Engineer/Drafter/Programmer for Precise Products Company, Lincoln, RI; Drafter for Tupperware Mold Development, North Smithfield, RI

Peter Alberg (right), at Hilti in Kaufering, Germany, with colleague Dr. J. Günther (left), and IEP intern Rhys Goff

Becoming a German IEP graduate opened many doors for my career, thus enabling me to take a job in Germany. Working at Hilti I have learned a whole different approach to development, stressing responsibility, self-confidence, patenting and technical skills.

Before Peter Alberg went off to Germany for his semester of study in Braunschweig and a six-month internship at Mercedes headquarters in Stuttgart, he came to my office with a concerned look on his face. He wanted to assure me that he was really looking forward to the year abroad, but wanted me to know at the same time that he was a Rhode Islander at heart and would not want to launch a career far from home once he had his degree. I told him that was not an issue. Our goal was to expand his educational horizons, and to provide the skills to work globally, whether here in Rhode Island or elsewhere, and to create corresponding opportunities. In no way were we trying to control where students would spend their lives. A year later, after a productive and rewarding year in Germany, Peter made another visit to my office, reminding me of our earlier conversation and letting me know cautiously that he had been rethinking his idea of working solely in Rhode Island. This time he wondered what the chances would be of finding a job in Germany and thus at least beginning his engineering career there. After letting him know that I was somehow not surprised, I helped him arrange three interviews with companies in Germany, and he returned from his trip with three very good offers (one U.S. based). Since that time (1998), Peter has been part of the research and development team of the German subsidiary of the Liechtenstein-based Hilti Corporation, a manufacturer of high-end drilling and cutting tools, as well as other devices and systems for the building industry, where he is now a Senior Design Engineer. His career start in Germany, which prior to his year abroad had not even been a mild consideration, led to a successful career with Hilti, a happy marriage to a Braunschweig classmate from the Czech

Republic and the birth of their two sons. Peter still is very close to his family and friends in Rhode Island, where he and his family often spend vacations, but Germany has become home.

Peter Alberg had come to the IEP somewhat late in his educational career. Though he attended mainly college-prep classes, Peter was intrigued with mechanical drawing as a high school student. This passion led him to Hall Institute in Pawtucket, RI where he earned certificates in both drafting and the new upcoming field of computer-aided drafting. His good academic record led directly to his first job at Tupperware Rhode Island. But after 2+ years in the mold design department, he realized he wanted to do more, though lacked the necessary background. As a result, he started attending classes part time at the Community College of Rhode Island, where he obtained Associate degrees in both Mechanical Engineering Technology and Engineering. During this time he left Tupperware (development relocated to Florida) and took a job at a small tool and die machine shop in Rhode Island, gaining valuable experience performing all sorts of engineering-related tasks. Working there was not only rewarding; it alerted him to the fact that he could do more. As a result, after 2 years, he decided to apply to the engineering program at URI where he would receive credit for most of the work done toward the Associate Degree. He hoped to earn his Bachelor's degree in mechanical engineering through two more years of study.

Peter had not known about the IEP until his interview with the URI College of Engineering's Assistant Dean Richard Vandeputte, who piqued his interest in taking a German course. Because he had regularly heard a lot about Germany from his immigrant grandmother, he had always wanted to learn some German, even if it was not a primary focus. To his own surprise, he found his URI German class and the language learning process to be enjoyable, so he continued the German curriculum, even though pursuing the IEP would mean extra time and a delay for continuing his career. His initial plan had been to earn the BS as fast as possible, so he could reenter the workforce with better chances for advancement.

Being a transfer student, Peter began his engineering studies at the Junior level. Starting German at that point would mean that he was two years behind any peers who would normally to go to Germany after the third academic year. In an attempt to catch up, he decided to enroll in URI's six-week German summer immersion program, the German Summer School of the Atlantic, where he completed an academic year's worth of German in six weeks, and where he became fully convinced that he could and would become a fluent speaker of the language and would do what was necessary to spend an academic year in Germany. Peter therefore completed the second year German program in the summer and the third year sequence in the next two semesters, thereby qualifying himself to spend the 1997-1998 year studying at the Technical University of Braunschweig and completing an internship with Daimler Benz. Unlike traditional IEP students, Peter spent his last academic year in Germany rather than his fourth. This would enable him to advance his language skills and complete an internship after receiving his engineering Bachelor of Science. He would then need just one additional semester in Rhode Island to complete both degrees.

To say that Peter's year in Germany was transformative, as we can clearly see by where it led him, is an understatement. Growing up in Pawtucket, Rhode Island, where his major fascination and professional goals were associated with drafting, the IEP "fell into my lap" and "took me by surprise," having never before dreamed that he might learn German, study in Germany, and intern in Stuttgart with one of the world's leading car manufacturers. Beyond that, the idea that he might launch a career three thousand miles from Rhode Island, marry a Czech woman and raise his family in Germany never even approached his radar screen. When asked what opportunities the IEP created for him, therefore, Peter's blunt response was: "What doors didn't it open for me!"

150

The year in Germany was definitely eye-opening for Peter who had heard a lot about the country from his grandmother as a child, and had of course learned a great deal through his language classes at URI. But he had no idea of the extent to which his year abroad would unveil a new world beyond Rhode Island.

Aside from the obvious differences like living and working abroad, the IEP path led me to my wife. We now have two lovely children who benefit greatly from our international experience. Within our household three languages are spoken and my children's fluency at a young age is breathtaking.

Braunschweig exposed him to the way engineering is taught at a German technical university, with its focus on high-level research, but it also exposed him to the attitudes and life style of German students, who tended to be older and more mature than American undergrads, as was he. As a foreign student taking additional German classes in Braunschweig, he also got to know many other students from all over the world, one of whom had come from the Czech Republic and would eventually become his wife! Peter furthermore took advantage of Braunschweig's central European location and learned to love travelling, visiting nearly all the western European countries.

The six months spent at Mercedes headquarters in the Stuttgart area were also transformative for Peter, whose engineering practice had been limited to Tupperware and other small firms in and around Rhode Island. He thrived at his internship in a Mercedes automatic transmission production plant with a focus on optimization and quality control. He tells us that he was given real responsibilities by his mentors and expected to bring value to the process. Here too he learned a great deal about German engineering, with its famed attention to quality and detail. His work was completed solely in German, meaning that his language skills, especially as they applied to the engineering workplace, advanced substantially. When he thus returned to Germany for job interviews a few months later, he was able to present himself in German as a professional engineer and secure two very good job offers.

Since 1998, Peter has been a practicing engineer at the principal location in Germany for Hilti AG, a global company based in Liechtenstein, with production in several countries and a sales reach to well over 100 nations worldwide. Today he is a senior design engineer for Hilti's famous drilling equipment, with responsibilities for the machines themselves. Anyone in the building industry knows that Hilti equipment is tops if there is a need to drill or cut concrete, stone, or metal. In his words: *I am presently responsible for component and subassembly development for various diamond drilling power tools. Present duties include development of concepts, simulation through calculation, part specification including drawing creation and material specification as well as production methods, and coordination with all other facets of product develop-*

152

ment (concurrent engineering).

Peter definitely views himself as a global engineer, since he works with team members from multiple locations, and works on the development of products for the global marketplace. German is the language of his office, but he is often called upon for his native English skills as they collaborate with vendors, suppliers, customers and other partners in Europe or other locations around the globe.

What can we learn from Peter Alberg?

1. Peter is most certainly one of the best examples of someone who learned through higher education and international study that he could reach personally and professionally far beyond his initial hopes, plans, and dreams. His international education experience opened doors and completely recast his life's plans. Given what he has accomplished personally and professionally and what he now represents as an American abroad, we can clearly argue the transformative power of a long-term international education experience. Peter Alberg had been a student with modest goals, which, though solid, were not tapping his full potential. The IEP experience introduced him to a much larger world, and gave him the inspiration and courage to reach higher.

2. As educators we learn once again from Peter how important it is that we reach out to and for talented young people and alert them to the importance and value of language and culture study in combination with their professional field. Had he not been alerted to the IEP and its opportunities by Assistant Dean Vandeputte, Peter would have stayed with his initial plan to complete the BS as quickly as humanly possible in order to return to the workforce. In short, the IEP and similar programs at other institutions must stay heavily focused on outreach programs not only to the secondary schools, but also to community colleges where many bright young engineers get their first start.

3. As with most cases in this study, we learn again from Peter Alberg the importance of "selling" the pragmatic value of second language learning. He had always had a mild interest in German due to the heritage of his family. But, when he went back to school to complete his BS, German would never have been part of his academic program had he not learned about the IEP and the chance to do a six-month internship with a company like Daimler Benz. He entered the German classroom and eventually majored in German because he could see that it would have a clear value, both professionally and personally. He was not required to learn German, and he did not follow through because of the vague ideals often used to justify language study. He did the work because he could see that it would offer extraordinary educational enrichment and far better career opportunities.

Peter defines the global engineer as: *someone with a technical background who has proven the ability to work in an international environment. For me this does not include someone who has no (or little) language experience who simply travels abroad for his company for meetings, etc. A global engineer does more than represent his country on foreign soil. A global engineer can integrate at another level with suppliers, vendors, and other engineers, often requiring (though not mandatory) the use of a foreign language. Knowledge of the cultures, habits, and local slang will not only facilitate any such meetings, but can help lay the groundwork for long lasting partnerships by building trust, even friendship.*

Peter Wiedenhoff

Born: Remscheid, North Rhine-Westphalia, Germany
Age: 32
Degrees: Master of Business Administration (MBA), University of Rhode Island, 2003; Diplom-Wirtschafts-ingenieur (Dipl.-Wirtsch.-Ing.), Technical University of Braunschweig, 2005; Dr.-Ing. (Doctorate in Engineering), Technical University of Braunschweig, 2011
Past Position: Associate Consultant, Boston Consulting Group, Munich, Germany, 2006-2011
Present Position: Senior Consultant, Boston Consulting Group, Munich, Germany

I believe that I have become a different person as a result of the IEP. The program really helped to broaden my horizon and to feel like a world citizen rather than a German. Since then I have visited numerous countries and made friends around the world.

Unlike the other IEP alumni in this study, Peter Wiedenhoff was not an undergraduate at URI, and he is not an American. He is, rather, a German citizen, who came to URI in 2002/2003 through the IEP exchange program with

155

the Technical University of Braunschweig and completed his MBA through provisions of the URI/Braunschweig dual degree program at the master's level. Given the fact that well over 500 students have been exchanged through the IEP, it is appropriate that a student coming to URI through the IEP exchange be included in this study. Peter is an excellent example of a European student who took advantage of the opportunity to prepare himself globally and has since built an impressive career as a technical and management consultant for clients across the globe.

The IEP has developed exchange relationships in each of its target countries, enabling IEP undergrads to study at partner schools in Germany, France, Spain, Mexico, and China for one semester before doing their professional six-month internships, and thus experiencing engineering abroad as it is taught and as it is practiced. The exchanges have each been developed on a one-to-one basis, with students fulfilling financial obligations at the home institution and then simply exchanging places. In the case of the Technical University of Braunschweig, students are given the opportunity to complete actual degrees at the host university through dual degree agreements at the master's and doctoral levels. Examples of URI students (Americans) completing the dual degree program are included in this volume in the discussions of Eric Sargent and Nika McManus.

German students coming to URI from Braunschweig quickly discovered the opportunity to complete master's level work. Given the fact that the traditional first degree at technical universities in Germany, simply known as the *Diplom*, is at the master's level, the Braunschweig students coming to URI had already achieved the equivalent of the BS in engineering and were prepared to jump immediately into coursework leading to the MS in an appropriate engineering field, or, as in the case of Peter Wiedenhoff, the URI intensive one-year MBA program. Since the signing of the dual degree agreement in 1997, 100 Braunschweig students have completed the MS in an engineering field and 64 have completed the MBA at URI.

Peter Wiedenhoff's degree program in Braunschweig (Wirtschaftsingenieurwesen) was comprised of both business and engineering with a focus on electrical engineering, and is approximately equivalent to American undergraduate degrees in both areas. Because his personal goals were set more on a career in business than in engineering, he decided to seek the MBA degree at URI rather than the MS in electrical engineering. He believed at the time that the combination of a German technical degree with an American MBA would provide excellent credentials for a career in global business. Indeed, it did help him to secure excellent internship opportunities with Bain & Company and Boston Consulting Group in Germany, as he was completing his Braunschweig degree, and, as we see from his current position with Boston Consulting, the combination did help him to find a position with one of the world's top management consulting companies. Peter joined BCG first as an Associate Consultant in 2006, after completing his *Diplom* at Braunschweig, before returning to Braunschweig for his doctorate and then rejoining BCG as a Senior Consultant in 2011.

Peter is a good example of someone eager to go the extra mile. Had he not opted to go to Rhode Island as an exchange student, he most likely could have completed his Braunschweig degree and found a position in Germany a year earlier. But he saw the exchange as an opportunity to live in the United States for a year, strengthen his English language skills, gain a deeper understanding of the American culture, and earn a coveted MBA degree. He believed, and rightly so, that a year abroad would enhance his qualifications and make him far more competitive for career opportunities at the higher end of the spectrum. In line with this perspective, he not only completed these steps, but also decided to take a leave from BCG and return to Braunschweig for his doctorate after his first two years with the company. Unlike the U.S., where doctoral studies tend to be more appropriate for academic positions or for higher level research, the doctorate in Germany is respected more broadly and is valued and indeed almost revered in the corporate world.

Peter took full advantage of his time at URI. In addition to his commitment to hard work and the earning of an MBA, he opted to live in the IEP House, thus assuring lots of contact with IEP students, faculty, and staff, and lots of interaction with native-speaking Americans. Peter is an outgoing and positive individual who participated regularly in the activities and management of the IEP House and thus established many friendships. He learned to love college basketball American style and still follows the progress of the URI Rams. He also bought a used Ford and was able to travel on weekends and during university vacations, visiting New England, New York City, Washington, DC, Toronto, Montreal, and so on. I remember well when he and two friends thought nothing of driving the Ford to Florida in January during winter break. In short, he took full advantage of his year in the U.S., both academically and otherwise.

Upon completion of his degrees from Braunschweig and URI, Peter secured his position with Boston Consulting Group at their Munich office, where he is now a Senior Consultant. Boston Consulting Group is a top global management consulting firm with locations across the globe and over 4800 employees. It describes itself as the world's leading advisor on business strategy with clients in all sectors and regions, and was ranked in second place on Fortune's 2011 best companies list. Peter works out of the 500-person Munich office. As an engineer with business expertise, he appropriately specializes in work with clients mainly in the renewable energy sector, which was the research focus of his doctoral dissertation.

In Peter's words: *I advise my clients' top management and develop business growth strategies, accompany enterprises undergoing organizational change, set up market models, evaluate investment opportunities, and define measures to ensure a client's target achievements. My daily work has a strong global focus. I collaborate with international colleagues and client team members on multinational case assignments, e.g. in India, Mexico, South*

158

Africa, the USA, etc. To provide an example: For the first six months of 2011, I have been working on a case assignment in India for an Indian wind turbine manufacturer.

To say that Peter's work is global is almost an understatement, and this is well illustrated with an example provided by him: *While the client's wind energy systems are produced in India, R&D for the blades and turbines is done in Europe, mainly in Germany, the Netherlands, and Denmark. As the main task of my project related to a performance improvement program, I travelled a lot between these four countries. An essential prerequisite for the success of the project was to bring people together from the different cultural backgrounds and to jointly redefine the interfaces of communication. As soon as people started to talk to each other and to look beyond their own country boundaries, we could continue to work on the content and jointly develop best practices for the whole value chain from development to production and delivery of wind energy systems.*

It is interesting to note Peter's response when asked about the benefits and advantages of his global education, his language skills, and his cross-cultural communication expertise. Rather than viewing these skills as something unusual or perhaps a supplement to his engineering background, which is sooner the typical American attitude, he points out that these were basic expectations for someone with his career aspirations in Germany. He does not believe that his career has advanced faster as a result of such skills. He argues, rather, that they were entry-level requirements. In other words, international experience, fluency in at least three languages (Peter speaks German, English, French, and Spanish), and a background in both business and engineering were the starting point for a position at a company like Boston Consulting Group in Munich. Given their clients' global locations, such a background is fundamental and mandatory, and he would not have his job without this skill set. To quote Peter: *As I am working in the field of business consulting, I can say that I would never have received an offer for my current job position without*

159

experience abroad. In fact, many companies nowadays require international exposure of the candidates for specific job positions.

Peter (top row, second on right) with his BCG team

When asked what he gained as a professional engineer from his exposure abroad, Peter spoke of the differences in the educational approach, especially for the MBA program. In his words: *The greatest learning from my exchange year comes from the practical orientation of the MBA studies at URI. While German schools are typically more theoretically and conceptually focused, the URI business college goes one step further and covers numerous case studies to actually apply the learning. This approach helped me a lot, especially during the first years of my professional career, to tackle tasks and problems in the right way. It made my career entry easier.*

Just as with our American IEP alumni, it is rewarding to remain in contact with former exchange students such as Peter Wiedenhoff. Their feedback enforces our belief that in-depth study abroad for at least one year provides excellent skills for today's global workplace.

While some of the IEP students from abroad have found ways to launch careers here in the United States, the majority have returned to their home country and have found very attractive and responsible positions, mostly with globally involved companies.

Did the year in Rhode Island affect Peter Wiedenhoff personally, and long-term? Because he already had travel experience in the U.S. before his year in Rhode Island and because he was two or three years older than the average URI IEP student going abroad, one might not expect the experience abroad to be quite as earth-shaking as for the Americans. Nevertheless, it was an extremely memorable and positive year, both professionally and personally, and he does not hesitate to praise its value. *Yes, I believe that I have become a different person as a result of the IEP. The program really helped to broaden my horizon and to feel like a world citizen rather than a German. Since then I have visited numerous countries and made friends around the world.* Among other things, Peter learned the love of travel during that year and the excitement of meeting and working with persons in many different national locations. Furthermore, he and his wife are now both avid vacation travelers, having in recent years visited countries in North and South America, Africa, and Asia.

While Peter was always an open-minded and outgoing person, he, like the American students, is among those who attribute his ability to "think bigger" and the confidence to reach for the challenge level to his experience abroad. As a bright and motivated student, we can be sure that he would have succeeded personally and professionally with or without the year abroad. However, he would not have been a candidate of interest for Boston Consulting Group and he most likely would not have made it to the first tier of global business. In his words: *The year really encouraged me to think bigger. While the step to go to Braunschweig made me aware of (job) opportunities beyond my hometown, my stay abroad at URI disclosed further, even more challenging options that I wanted to address after*

161

my return to Germany. So the idea to work for a global consulting company really evolved throughout that year.

What can we learn from Peter Wiedenhoff?

1. Peter's case teaches us the degree to which international education, including multilingualism, must become the norm rather than the exception. For him it was clear from the beginning that global work requires global education, and that his career options would be limited without it. For the majority of American engineering students and faculty, this is unfortunately still not obvious.

2. Peter shows us as well how much would be lost if the IEP were strictly a one-way arrangement, and did not include the interaction of American students with their peers from abroad. Both learn so much from each other, and are educated as they grow to understand the assumptions and points of views of their partners. Having students like Peter in our IEP living and learning community is enormously helpful for the American students before they go abroad. It is one of the earlier steps in what becomes a life-long networking program, first among students, then among professionals, from country to country. It is gratifying to note that Peter still maintains contact with several of his URI friends, meeting them sometimes in the U.S., and sometimes in Germany.

3. Peter's case also illustrates the degree to which IEP students develop confidence and calculated risk-taking skills through their international education. For Germans, who are famous for their *Heimatgebundenheit* (ties to home), it was no doubt a big step to leave his hometown in the Rhineland for Braunschweig, but then an even bigger step to leave Germany for a year in Rhode Island. Peter points out that each step made the next one easier, and that with each step, his own personal expectations of himself grew. The personal and professional outcome for him was a highly desirable position in an

absolutely top-tier global consulting firm.

4. Peter helps us also to understand what it is that American and German professionals can learn from each other. He praises the practical and pragmatic approach of the case study method and contrasts it with the far more theoretical and detail-driven approach of the German universities. Here again he gained insights and experience which would equip him to deal with real-world issues facing managerial consultants and the need for quick solutions. It is clear that Germans and Americans often take different approaches to problem solving and that our international engineers, whether German or American, must gain an appreciation for both.

As is appropriate for his position, Peter chooses to define the global consultant rather than the global engineer: *A global consultant must be flexible to work in different countries and deal with various topics from different practice areas. As a global consultant, you need to be prepared to work closely together with colleagues and clients from different cultural backgrounds.*

Conclusions

The purpose of this study has been to examine the lives and careers of professionally active graduates of the University of Rhode Island International Engineering Program (IEP), with hopes of being better able to understand and more clearly define the outcomes and value of their international education experiences. What did these alumni learn through their foreign study and internship program that they would not have learned otherwise? What skills did they acquire as a result of the overall IEP curriculum and what role did these skills play in their career advancement and in their personal lives? Though each of our fifteen cases is unique and thus differs to a degree from the others, we have found very clear commonalities among this group, which will enable us to draw several conclusions and refine our understanding of the goals and priorities of a program such as the IEP.

1. Confirming What We Have Claimed: It is important to note that the International Engineering Program has consistently put forth and maintained a set of goals and standards and has always been confident that its students were benefitting from their language and culture study parallel to the engineering curriculum and their time spent abroad. Feedback from our students, from faculty abroad, and from internship mentors has always been positive for the great majority of cases. A far larger group of IEP alumni was surveyed in 2006 by IEP German Professor Walter von Reinhart, with responses from approximately 100 former students. He was able to document widespread satisfaction with the IEP. 100% confirmed that they would even recommend the IEP, its study abroad and internship "to their children or best friend!" Von Reinhart confirmed furthermore that very close to 100% of the grads had found a job within six months of graduation, with approximately two thirds being placed with a global company or a company doing at least part of its work globally. The great majority reported that their international experience and second degree played a significant role in the job interview process.

The current study represents the first time that we have approached a set of alumni after several years in the workplace with a detailed set of questions regarding the skills acquired through the IEP and the direct relevance of these skills to their careers. Any evaluation of the program, such as student self-assessment surveys and pre- and post-study and /or internship interviews, has limited results at the student level and can only be validated longitudinally, after some years of professional experience. It is one thing, for example, to attempt to evaluate a concept such as cross-cultural competency through inventories such as the IDI (Intercultural Development Index) or role playing techniques during the student years; it is quite another to assess such a concept based upon years of personal professional experience in the global workplace. Given the twenty-four year history of the IEP and the sizeable group of alumni active in their careers, the Rhode Island faculty is now in a unique position nationally to be able to raise questions regarding the impact of an in-depth global education for engineers. There are several other international engineering education pro-grams with a significant history, but none with this time span who have demanded a full language degree next to their engineering curriculum and a full year abroad.

Historically, the IEP leadership has, of course, strongly promoted the value of foreign study and professional practice abroad for engineers. It has furthermore believed that the full appreciation of another culture cannot be attained without a long-term stay of minimally two semesters in the country of that culture, with all work done in the national language. Bilingualism has many benefits. Beyond the deeper cultural access, it provides a better

165

understanding of language itself, including a greater appreciation of one's own native tongue. We have argued additionally that engineers cannot appreciate the culture of their discipline abroad without access to the language in which the work is practiced. Whether in the laboratory, on the shop floor, or in the university dormitory, if we really want to know how the Germans, for example, approach or solve a problem, or how they really feel about issues large or small, then we need to hear them express their opinions in their own environment, in their own language. They may have very good English skills, but they do their thinking and their day-to-day work in their native tongue.

It is not a surprise to us that students return from their year abroad with a far greater appreciation of the value of their new language, and even gratitude for our insistence upon language learning. Nor is it a surprise in this study to hear pride being expressed in their ongoing use of their new language and the value of bilingualism in their careers. Cases such as Christina Smith, Ana Franco, Jesse Schneider, Eric Sargent, Matt Zimmerman, and Sonia Gaitan illustrate very clear professional advantages as a result of their bilingualism due to the clear need in their careers for French, German, Spanish and Portuguese. For Eric Sargent, Jesse Schneider, Dan Fischer, and others in this study, knowing German is not an option or a valuable supplement, but rather a prerequisite for their jobs. But there are those too, such as Ana Franco, Jesse Schneider, Sonia Gaitan, and Matt Zimmerman who have become language learning enthusiasts, taking on the study of new languages, whether for personal or professional reasons, or just for the fun of it. Who says that engineers are not good language learners?!

Another often observed outcome of study abroad for IEP students is the love of travel. IEP students are in many cases first-generation college students and not the offspring of well-travelled families. Indeed, most IEP students do not possess a passport before preparing for their two semesters abroad. But any squeamishness regarding travel to unknown places changes when they suddenly find them-selves in Europe, in easy reach of cities like Prague, Berlin,

Rome, Paris, or Amsterdam. As a result we read in their diaries about bargain travel with the *Deutsche Bahn*, weekend $35 flights with Ryan Air, running with the bulls in Pamplona (!), going to Copenhagen to join a road race, or even making journeys to the pyramids in Egypt. Ana Franco sums this up well in her comments to me. Beyond her new passion for language and culture, she reports that the IEP gave her the "travel bug": *Having the opportunity to travel through Europe for a year and then for 6 weeks in China opened a new world for me. I make the effort to go on a trip (non work-related) somewhere outside the US at least once a year. I have gone to the Dominican Republic, Machu Picchu Peru, the Bahamas, and Greece this year.*

Our study also reinforces the argument that mobility and cultural flexibility are clear outcomes of the program. It is astonishing to note the amount of work-related travel involved in the routine professional life of the fifteen alums in this study. In contacting our project participants over the course of 2011 by e-mail, Skype, or telephone, I was always able to find them, but it was never clear where I would find them. Ryan Courneyor travelled throughout North America, Europe, the Middle East, Africa, and Asia during his time with Bentley Systems; Eric Sargent might be at any given time in New Jersey, South Carolina, Detroit or Munich; Jesse Schneider might be in Washington, Detroit, or Munich; Christina Smith could be found in Rhode Island, Wichita or Germany; Matt Zimmerman in Rhode Island, Italy, France or Monte Carlo; Ana Franco could be found in Rochester, New York, the Middle East, Greece, or Latin America; and Peter Wiedenhoff, while based in Munich, may be found anywhere between North America and South Asia. It is clear that engineering graduates without foreign travel or study experience would be very much at a disadvantage in today's global workplace. Being sent, for example, to China with no previous exposure to global travel or work with colleagues in other cultural settings would be intimidating at the very least, and potentially devastating.

IEP faculty members have also argued over the years that in-depth experience abroad at both a technical university and then as an intern with a company in the same culture provides insight into the engineering culture of that society and therewith to an understanding that the basis for engineering decisions is not uniform from country to country. Technology is subject to different cultural, social and political considerations and is often derived from different value systems. This is certainly born out and reinforced by the participants in this study. Eric Sargent, for example, who completed graduate study in both Rhode Island and Germany and wrote his thesis under the supervision of engineers at BMW headquarters in Munich, is now in a unique position to mediate between the BMW engineering groups in Germany and the United States. He can explain to the Americans how and why the German engineers are taking a given approach; likewise he can explain to the Germans that a BMW automobile is experienced differently in North America than in Europe. While Germans, for example, are far more fascinated by technology and the ability to drive 150 mile per hour on the *Autobahn*, Americans might be sooner concerned about the air conditioning function in the Texas climate, the maneuverability in the snow of Vermont, or the position and quality of the cup holder.

We have also argued throughout the history of the IEP that in-depth study abroad provides a life-long reference point or basis of comparison as one approaches many aspects of life and work, whether at home or abroad. When returning home from their year away, IEP students have a new sense of a broad range of societal issues, impacting their views of environmental stewardship, health care, higher education, immigration, public transportation, the use of natural resources, and so on. IEP students learn that Americans cannot live in a national bubble, but are vitally interconnected within a global network of nations, all dependent on each other to one degree or another. In short, returning students view themselves and their world quite differently, having lived and worked abroad for a full year.

168

This new-found knowledge will always be there as a direct influence on their thinking as they work, as they raise their children, as they read a newspaper, as they make their business and technical decisions.

It is important to note that these positive outcomes of the IEP model have been clearly endorsed by the private sector, with whom we collaborate so closely. The hard-core facts of our graduates' immediate employment in globally operating companies, as well as their global responsibilities, speak for themselves. Furthermore, in a recent survey[11] asking about the language and cross-cultural needs of Rhode Island-based global companies, CEO's confirmed the need to have multilingual engineers who can communicate with clients abroad as well as interact effectively with the more and more diverse workforce whom they might be supervising. The respondents spoke, among other things, of missed opportunity costs due to the lack of language skills, as well as the need for "ambassadors" who can foster the bonding process between parent companies and their subsidiaries abroad.

2. Recognizing Other Valuable Outcomes: Certainly this study reinforces our original thinking about study and work abroad, e.g., the benefits of exposure to another culture, learning another language, developing an appreciation for other cultural perspectives, learning to be mobile, viewing and experiencing difference in so many aspects of life and society. Our fifteen participants are all in agreement with these aforementioned concepts. At the same time, however, they have also stressed certain benefits of their educational experience which we have not traditionally identified or have not brought to the forefront of our thinking. These relate very much to personal growth at a critical stage in life and to the **development of soft skills** which they view as some of the most important keys to their own success.

---

[11] Conducted by Erin Papa, Coordinator of the URI Chinese Language Flagship Program, graduate assistant Robynn Butler, and Dr. Sigrid Berka, IEP Executive Director, in preparation for the Rhode Island Language Summit meeting conducted in Providence, RI, December 7, 2011.

Most of our project participants have pointed out that the year spent abroad helped them develop important **problem solving skills** by virtue of the fact that they were required while away to address daily issues of both lesser and greater magnitude independently. University systems abroad expect a far greater maturity of students than does the American system and are consequently less nurturing. The U.S system tends to spoon-feed the learning process and provide support for just about any conceivable problem, while parents often hover in the background making sure that their child is not being ignored or mistreated. Most IEP students, therefore, are truly on their own for the first time when abroad, doubly challenged by an environment well outside their comfort zones. The language and culture, the banking system, the housing system, the traffic system, the university system, the diet, attitudes toward America, and so forth are all different than in the United States and each encounter has its own learning curve. Students admit readily to their culture shock in the beginning and tell us that each day brings a new challenge and a new problem to be solved, complicated by the fact that everything is to be done in a language which they are now generally using on a daily basis for the first time. All of this becomes more complex in the second part of the year when students separate from their peers and move on to their professional internship on their own, in a new city, with a new housing situation, responsibility for their own meals, a new set of strangers, and new yet-to-be-defined responsibilities in a company where they have not worked before. Help can no longer come from parents or friends and support from the home university is limited. Truly, they are young, would-be professionals on their own for the first time and very much outside their comfort zones.

Some might describe this as overly demanding and possibly even cruel, which explains why so many American programs abroad are heavily sheltered and designed to function much like the education at home. Yet, the IEP students themselves thrive as a result of this experience abroad and, especially in looking back, recognize the year as a huge personal growth period, resulting in a **leap in self-confidence** and the ability to take on problems as they occur.

To quote Sareh Rajaee: *The IEP experience, especially my year abroad, helped me build confidence in my interpersonal communication skills, in my independence, and in myself as an individual. The IEP showed me what I am capable of, and I am now a stronger, happier, and more independent person because of it.*

Or Daniel Fischer: *The IEP put me in situations that I would not have experienced in the U.S. In that sense, you grow and learn how big your comfort zone is and what you can do when you find yourself in situations on the border of or outside of this zone.*

Or John DiMuro: *I'm a much different person as a result of the IEP. The world is a lot smaller and my ambitions are a lot larger. Challenges don't look as daunting, and as a result, I'm more willing to provide my opinion or step forward to work on a project.*

Related to the growth in the ability to accept challenges and solve problems independently is the tendency noted among our project participants **to "think big,"** to reach for the top, and **to take calculated risks**, i.e., **to dare to go the extra mile**. Though one might argue that such character traits or abilities are buried in genetics, in the home environment, or are due to collective life experiences, our alums have attributed much of their confidence and risk taking capabilities to the overall IEP experience. Sareh Rajaee's quote above relates to her jump to medical school from the IEP and her belief that she could, for example, dare to earn a Harvard Masters in Public Health along side her Brown MD. This once reserved and shy student then competed and won a residency position in vascular surgery at non other than Yale. Sharon Ruggieri, who came to URI as a very reserved young woman, had the courage by graduation time to turn down a position with a global jet engine manufacturer in the belief that she would win a Fulbright year in Mexico. A year later she then turned down a position with Nissan, confident that she would be admitted

171

to the MIT Sloan School of Management. As Sharon writes: *At the IEP I started to gain confidence in myself and as a consequence I began to succeed. As a result of the opportunities at the IEP, I began to believe I could reach even higher and this led me to the Fulbright program and later to MIT. Before the IEP my universe was limited to my state; now my education and professional career has no borders.*

Matt Zimmerman, who had the courage to start his own company rather than accept job offers with guaranteed salaries, also recognizes that his confidence and belief that he could succeed as an entrepreneur, were bolstered by his IEP experience. *The IEP enforced my belief that I can achieve great things and implement big ideas. Students need to see that reiterated many times. The IEP gave me the chance to live in another country during my college career. That is an experience that makes one think differently.*

Risk taking and the expansion of personal goals are qualities promoted by the IEP from the very first day of the freshman year, which then culminate in the very critical year abroad. In a sense, the IEP itself may be described as a risk. Students are being asked to devote an extra year, pay extra tuition for one semester, take on the task of learning a new language, and to leave their home comfort zone for an entire year. Accepting that challenge, which they hope will yield advantages for their careers and their salaries, is not for everyone and many find it simply too much work and/or too intimidating, especially as they get close to the year abroad. By taking this risk, however, every IEP student acquires skills and accrues advantages which are often unseen or even unimagined at the outset. One of the larger lessons is the discovery that "daring to go the extra mile" will open doors to opportunities that would otherwise not be there.

Eric Sargent, who almost dropped out of high school, took that risk by jumping into the IEP, which led from one risk to another, but ultimately to a high-level job with BMW that was once just a dream. *I can say with certainty that I would not be anywhere near where I am today, if not for the IEP.*

172

Ryan Cournoyer, who held a very secure position with a large global company, had the courage to transition recently to a young and small, four-person company, which will, he believes, provide a new set of challenges and greater long-term rewards. He knows he is taking a chance, but he has the courage to do so, and, as he tells us: *I was presented with an opportunity that was definitely more risky (less financial backing, but higher reward potentials). Having the international background and experience gave me the confidence to move forward and take that risk.*

Johnathan DiMuro, who originally had URI on his list of schools as a clear last resort, took the chance with his local state university after learning about the IEP. Four years later, after his year abroad and an expanded view of the world, he decided he was in a good position to compete for a Truman Fellowship, which ultimately took him to the Master's Program in Engineering for Sustainable Development at Cambridge University in England. Now he finds himself in a "dream position" as Project Manager for a major sustainability initiative at Dow Chemical in partnership with The Nature Conservancy. Like others in this volume, the IEP released a chain of events that enabled him to reach higher at each stage. As he tells us: *I'm a much different person as a result of the IEP. The world is a lot smaller and my ambitions are a lot larger.*

Another outcome of the IEP, as illustrated by this group of fifteen, relates to **a shared personal bond, friendships, personal relationships,** marriages, and ultimately, quality of life. There are those like Chris and Mike Smith who met as IEP students and subsequently married, and there are those like Jesse Schneider, Dan Fischer, and Peter Alberg who met their spouses while working or studying abroad. But there are also those like Ana Franco and Sonia Gaitan who share their lives, both professional and personal, with a large number of IEP alumni through Facebook and other social venues. And there are those who like to meet when possible, travel together and support each other in all aspects of life. A significant "culture of giving back" has emerged amongst the IEP alumni leading to the success of a recent fund-drive which raised approximately $350,000.

Though I would hardly recommend the IEP to students as a means of finding a spouse, it is nevertheless valid to note that lives are changed through a long-term, in-depth experience abroad and that those who have had that experience gladly associate with others who have shared and can appreciate that. The international dimension provides a strong common bond and offers a reason to be together and identify with one another.

3. **Implications (Lessons) for Higher Education**: If we accept the messages from our group of fifteen alumni regarding the outcomes and value of their inter-national engineering education, then it is incumbent upon us to ask what this means for the design and form of our existing programs. This is especially so for the IEP, since we have learned that some of the most powerful outcomes of our own program, such as growth in personal confidence and the ability to "think big," are not addressed in our curriculum, in our advising, or in our recruitment procedures. But the message from this group also has implications nationally as we work with colleagues across the country to understand and define the best approaches for educating engineers to work globally.

a. Reconsidering Program Evaluation: Certainly we are obliged to use whatever tools we have in the bag for evaluating the progress of our students. We need to be confident that our instruction, whether in engineering or language study, is sound and meets standards on a global level. This we can do by working with colleagues at home and at our partner institutions abroad and by using whatever measurement tools have been developed, such as the ACTFL Oral Proficiency guidelines and examinations, or possibly the IDI (Intercultural Development Index). At the same time, we need to be aware of and make our students aware of the less measureable benefits of the program which will be of great value to them in the future. It is probably not feasible to measure progress in personal self-confidence, the ability to solve problems large or small, the ability to

174

take calculated risks, or to "think big" when given the chance. It is probably not feasible to test the ability to find the right lifelong partner or to choose a living environment and life style in which future children can thrive and be happy. But, if we are to believe our fifteen participants in this project, their international study and time spent abroad had an enormous effect for them on these very qualities. We therefore need to be far more aware of these sides of the program and their implications for the lives of our students and their potential for success. We need to feel confident about informing students and potential students about the life-changing characteristics of programs such as the IEP. This is not to say that our fifteen students would not have achieved success or personal satisfaction without the IEP. It is to say, however, that they have done so in a greatly expanded context and with a much broader perspective than if they had done an engineering degree without the international component. The range of opportunities available to them, as an outcome of the value added by the international experience, grew substantially as a result of the IEP.

b. Expanding the Message to Potential Students: Throughout this series of case studies, we have been reminded of the importance of student recruitment at the high school level. Sharon Ruggieri, Sonia Gaitan, Eric Sargent, and Daniel Fischer learned about the IEP as a result of presentations at their schools, and might or might not have joined the program otherwise. While it is, therefore, clear that this form of marketing is of extreme importance as a means for spreading the word, we also need to adapt our presentations along with other marketing tools to tell the full story of the benefits of an in-depth global engineering education. We need to share the stories of graduates such as those presented in this volume and encourage young high school students to "think big," to stretch their imaginations about what they can achieve in their lives and to jump into a program that can truly change their lives. It is not just a matter of ensuring a job after graduation or chances of a better salary; it is a matter of expanding one's world view, of being able to expand one's personal potential and being able to make a greater contribution to our globalized society.

c. The Structure and Nature of Programs Abroad: If we explore the range of study abroad opportunities for engineering students, we see immediately that there is little consistency and little agreement regarding structure and nature. There are those who send their students for a three-week study tour; those who would send their students for at least a year, and there are those who feel the goals can be accomplished online without any physical presence abroad. There is also no agreement regarding curricular structure. Some send their students abroad to take classes taught in English by accompanying faculty, thereby guaranteeing the same quality as the home curriculum and no loss of time toward graduation; some, such as Georgia Tech in France, establish their own branches abroad, functioning as off-campus centers for their own systems and as profit-making centers, available to their own students and guest students from the host country; some, such as Purdue University, send their students for research experiences with students at partner universities in countries abroad; some, such as WPI, send their students abroad to complete technical projects under supervision of home faculty; others send their students for language and culture study experiences; others, such as URI, send their students to participate mainly in the culture, in the language, and in the curriculum of the host university abroad; and others, again such as URI, send their students to professional internship experiences with partnering global companies abroad.

We have learned from this participant group that being sent abroad for a full year to be immersed in a language and culture experience without the day-to-day handholding of the American system was of enormous value to them, not only for the measureable growth of their language skills and the completion of courses taught in another language, but in terms of personal growth, evolving from the challenge of taking on both small and large problems in an unfamiliar environment outside their comfort zones. Another byproduct of this year of personal discovery is the resulting courage and desire to substantially raise the bar for their own personal goals and aspirations.

The fifteen alums in this project all speak of this year abroad as a period of enormous personal and professional growth and see it as the most important part of their undergraduate program. This is not to say that there is little value in a short-term or highly sheltered experience, but the outcomes most praised by our alumni provide clear evidence that they have gained significant benefits that would not have come through a program designed especially for Americans and compressed into a summer or winter break. The development of language skills in country, the experience of engineering education as practiced in a technical university abroad, the appreciation of the way engineering is done in another cultural context and the understanding of the values driving technology decisions cannot be reached in a matter of weeks. Our group, therefore, strongly reinforces the IEP's commitment to a full year abroad, after at least three years of preparation technically, linguistically, culturally, and personally.

d. The Role and Definition of a Liberal Arts Education: In his interviews with me, Ryan Cournoyer spoke of the value of a liberal arts education for professionals in today's global workplace. He argued that employers welcome engineers with stronger writing and verbal skills, with global experience, languages other than English, and an appreciation for cultural difference, history, and current affairs. For Ryan, this breadth and depth was developed for him through the IEP and is thus a very important rationale and selling point for the program. Similar arguments were made by others in our participant group, several of whom had reservations about engineering as an overly narrow course of study. Chris Petersen Smith, for example, who is today very much a successful practicing engineer, tells us she may never have become an engineer if she could not have pursued her technical studies in combination with her interest in language and culture. She thrived in exercising both sides of her brain. Her course of study gave her the background to not only work globally, but to understand and appreciate difference, whether from national, disciplinary, or personal perspectives and to function as a mediator and bridge across the many divides.

The messages from the participants in this study certainly justify the IEP's linkage of the engineering curriculum with the liberal arts. In a sense, however, they go far beyond that. A close look at the long-term outcomes of such a cross-disciplinary program and the roles that these alumni play in today's society suggest that it is time for educators to reconsider what we mean by a liberal arts education. If we can argue that engineers need a broader educational background to include language and culture study and in-depth experience abroad, should we not also argue that liberal arts majors in the traditional sense are incomplete without an adequate background in science and technology? If we truly live in a global age, in which the disciplines are indeed intersecting on so many levels, and believe that this is the justification for globalizing engineering education, should not majors in all disciplines be expected to acquire global skills? I would argue that our fifteen cases provide a good model for the liberally educated young professional. They are technically savvy and competent, open-minded, good communicators, mobile, flexible, appreciative and accepting of difference, intellectually curious, entrepreneurial, and long-term learners. However we might quibble about definitions, and educators are very skilled at that, it would be hard to argue that the fifteen IEP alumni represented in this study are not good examples of liberally educated global citizens.

About the Author

John M. Grandin is Professor Emeritus of German and Director Emeritus of the International Engineering Program at the University of Rhode Island, an interdisciplinary curriculum, through which students complete simultaneous degrees (BA and BS) in German, French, Spanish, or Chinese, and in an engineering discipline. Grandin has received numerous awards for his work combining languages and engineering, including the Federal Cross of Honor (First Class) from the Federal Republic of Germany, the Award for Educational Innovation from ABET, and the Michael P. Malone Award for Excellence in International Education from NASULGC, the National Association of State Universities and Land Grant Colleges, the American Association of Teachers of German (AATG) Outstanding Educator Award; the DAAD Alumni Association Award for International Exchange, and the Association of Departments of Foreign Languages (ADFL) Award for Distinguished Service in the Profession. He has published widely on such cross-disciplinary initiatives and has been the principle investigator for several funded projects related to the development of the International Engineering Program. Grandin also founded and organized the Annual Colloquium on International Engineering Education, bringing together university faculty and business representatives each year to promote a more global engineering education nationally (http://uri.edu/iep). For additional articles by Grandin on the University of Rhode Island International Engineering Program, see:

"German and Engineering: An Overdue Alliance," Die Unterrichtspraxis, No. 22 (1989), pp. 146-152.

"Deutsch für Ingenieure: Das Rhode Island Programm," in Das Jahrbuch Deutsch als Fremdsprache, Vol. 15, (Fall 1989), pp. 297-306.

"Developing Internships in Germany for International Engineering Students," Die Unterrichtspraxis, No. 2 (1991), pp. 209-214.

"The International Engineering Internship Program at the University of Rhode Island," with Kristen Verducchi, in The Journal of Chemical Engineering Education," May 1996, pp. 126-129.

"Educating Engineers for the Global Workplace: A Study of Cross-Cultural Issues'" with Eric W. Dehmel, Journal of Language for International Business, Vol 8, Nr. 2 (1997), pp. 1-15.

"German and Engineering - ein interdisziplinäres Programm an der University of Rhode Island" with Doris Kirchner, in Wirtschaftsdeutsch International: Zeitschrift für sprachliche und interkulturelle Wirtschaftskommunikation, WDi 1/99, pp. 109-119.

"German and Engineering at the University of Rhode Island: Preparing Students for the Global Workplace," with Jennifer Dail, in Lernwelten: Eine Zeitschrift des Goethe-Instituts für Deutschlehrende in den USA, Heft 3, January-August 2000, pp. 9-10.

"Globalization and Its Impact on the Profession," in Realizing Our Vision of Languages for All, ed. Audrey Heining-Boynton, American Council on the Teaching of Foreign Languages, 2005.

"Preparing Engineers for the Global Workplace: The University of Rhode Island," in Proceedings of the Annual Meeting of the American Society for Engineering Education," June 2006.

"Preparing Engineers for the Global Workplace: The University of Rhode Island," in the Online

Journal for Global Engineering Education, Volume 1, Issue 1, Fall 2006.

"International Dual Degrees at the Graduate Levels: The University of Rhode Island and the Technische Universität Braunschweig," Proceedings of the ASEE Annual Conference, Honolulu, Hawaii, June 2007.

"International Dual Degrees at the Graduate Levels: The University of Rhode Island and the Technische Universität Braunschweig," in the *Online Journal for Global Engineering Education,* Volume 3, Issue 1, Fall 2008.

"Why Learn Another Language if the Whole World Speaks English?" in English as the Global Language: Perspectives and Implications, ed. S. Rajagopalan, the Icfai University Press, 2007.

Grandin, J.M. and Hirleman, E.D. "Educating Engineers as Global Citizens: A Call for Action", Report of the National Summit Meeting on the Globalization of Engineering Education, March, 2009. In print or accessed at http://digitalcommons.uri.edu/ojgee/vol4/iss1/

Grandin, J., Hedderich, N., "Intercultural Competence in Engineering," in Deardorff, Darla, The Sage Handbook of Intercultural Competence, Sage, 2009, pp. 362-373.